African and Caribbean Cookbook

Book 2

Tales and Recipes from the Motherland

Tales and Recipes from the Motherland

Share the experience and taste ... with us

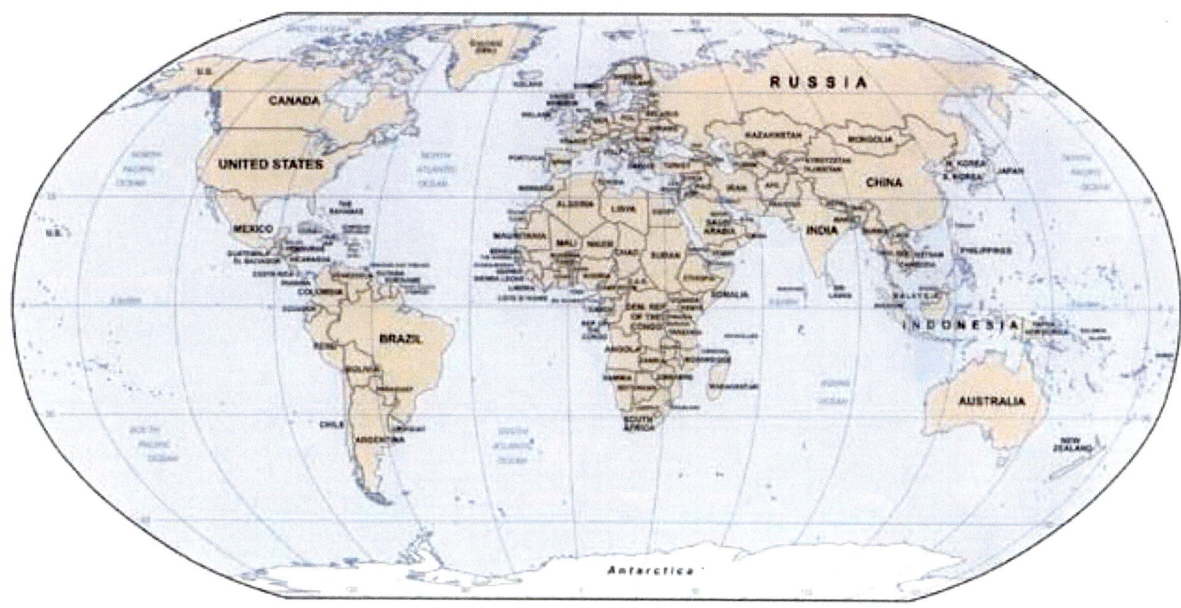

Maps from THE WORLD FACTBOOK

This book is to raise awareness and funds for further education of disadvantaged African and Caribbean children in the UK

Published May 2016 by Fast-Print Publishing

ISBN: 978-178456-348-6

Copyright © 2016 Dr Mrs Pamela Ayewoh-Bernard, MBE/The Multi-Heritage Organisation Limited

Bedford, England, UK

info@multi-heritageorg.co.uk

All Rights Reserved. No part of this book may be reproduced in any form, by photocopying or by electronic or mechanical means, including information storage or retrieval systems, without permission in writing from the copyright owner of this book. This book is not intended to give any legal, financial and/or medical advice to the readers.

A catalogue record for this book is available from the British Library

For information about special discounts for bulk purchases, please contact The Multi-Heritage Organisation Limited.

Health warning: Please be health-conscious when trying new ingredients and follow cooking instructions.

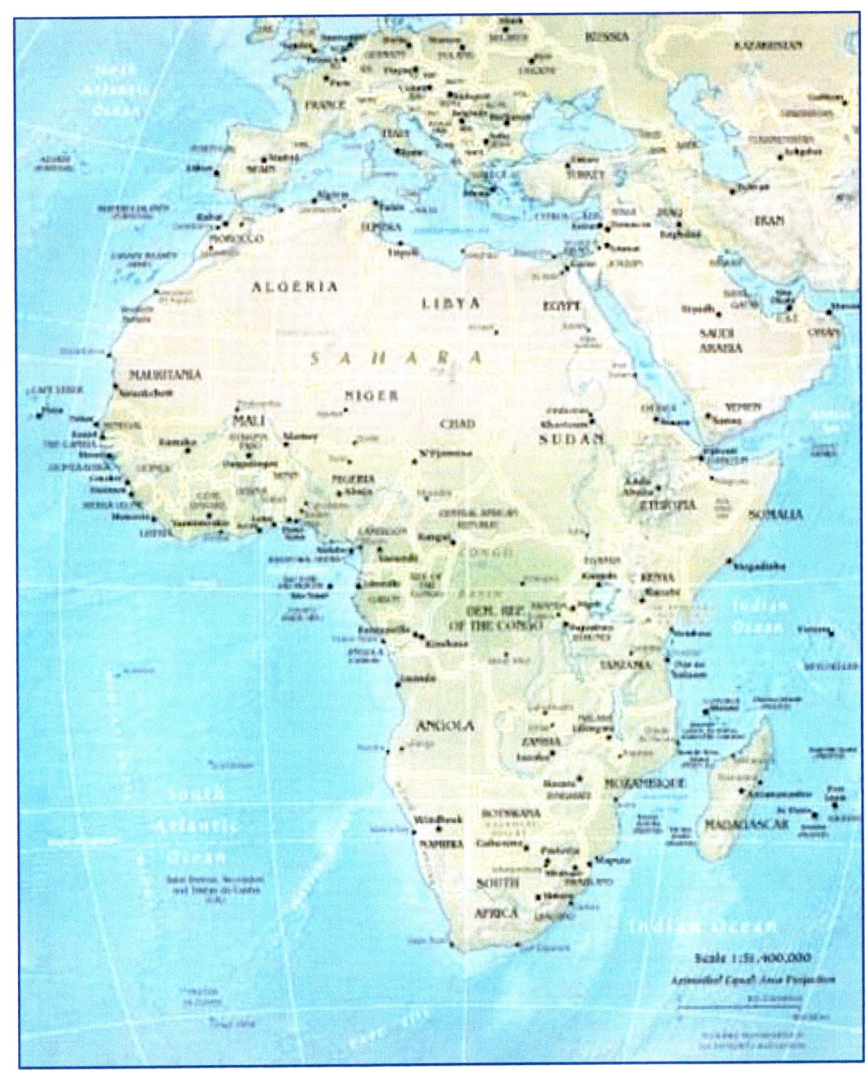

Participants

Mrs Carol Allen
Mr Emmanuel Amadi
Mrs Michele Balach-Ali
Mrs Folasade Bamgbala
Mrs Juliette Dickson
Mrs Aderonke Fadayiro
Mrs Pauline Garriques
Mrs Charmaine Gonera
Mrs Wema Grant
Ms Stella Idehen
Chief Matthew Iria
Mrs Hannah Jolaoso
Mrs Deborah Joseph-Edoyobi
Mrs Sissi Lungwa
Mrs Lilian Martins
Ms Lola MK
Mrs Maryam Muazu
Mrs Gertrude Chulu Nyoni
Mrs Mary Bolanle Odoi
Mrs Adesuwa Omoregie Ogie
Mrs Omosefe Ohirein
Mrs Marie-Rose Omokhodion
Mr Opoku Opare
Mr John OQuaye
Mrs Laurel Oronsaye
Mr Philip Otubanjo
Mrs Bibi Owusu-Shadbolt
Mrs Abiola Reis
Mrs Modupe Olanibi Robinson
Mrs Yemisi Siwoku
Mrs Valerie Taiwo
Ms Fay Taylor
Mrs Regina Tributh
Mrs Cathrine Ward

Thank you all for being part of this Project
Dr Mrs Pamela Ayewoh-Bernard, MBE

To
Our Children
&
Gratefulness to our Mothers

Contents

Participants 5

Contents 7

Introduction 9

Project Team 9

Foreword 10

Measurements 11

Mama Fry Stew Chicken *[Jamaica]* 12

Igbo Ogbono-Okra Soup with Eba *[Nigeria]* 14

Fried Chicken/Fish/Rice & Irish favourite *[Grenada]* 16

Grandma's Memory Pancake *[Nigeria]* 18

Afang/Ugu and Edikaikong Soup *[Nigeria]* 20

Yam and Liver Stew *[Nigeria]* 22

"Dutty Girl" *[Jamaica]* 24

Mupunga Une Dovi Ne Huku *[Zimbabwe]* 26

Caribbean Fried Snapper *[Jamaica]* 28

Banga Soup *[Nigeria]* 30

Esan Ogbono Soup with Pounded Yam *[Nigeria]* 32

Egusi Soup with Pounded Yam *[Nigeria]* 34

African Salad & Owerri Vegetable Soup *[Nigeria]* 36

Fumbua *[D R Congo]* 38

Ayamase *[Nigeria]* 40

Yoruba Okra Soup *[Nigeria]* 42

Suya/Tsire *[Nigeria]* 44

Zambia Family Meal *[Zambia]* 46

Yoruba Vegetable Soup *[Nigeria]* 48

Boiled Yam and Owoh Sauce *[Nigeria]* 50

Healthier Jollof Rice *[Nigeria]* 52

Poisson Braisé *[Ivory Coast]* 54

Palm Soup *[Ghana]* 56

Jollof Fried Rice *[Ghana]* 58

Coconut Rice *[Nigeria]* 60

Ewedu Soup with Eba *[Nigeria]* 62

ETO *[Ghana]* 64

Aroma Mix *[Nigeria]* 66

Ila-asepo *[Nigeria]* 68

Frejon and Akara – Yoruba style *[Nigeria]* 70

Akara – Eastern Nigeria Style *[Nigeria]* 72

Saturday Soup *[Barbados]* 76

Cameroon Pepper Soup *[Cameroon]* 78

Rice with Peanut Butter and Relish *[Zimbabwe]* 80

Glossary 82

Introduction

In 2011, we wrote the first African and Caribbean Cookbook to celebrate Black History Month and it was widely embraced. However, the most significant effect was on our children who welcomed the Cookbook and have since used the book to learn and prepare a variety of African and Caribbean dishes.

This has prompted me to compile a second book incorporating dishes from more African and Caribbean countries. We will continue to encourage our children and inspire more people to share the experience and taste of African and Caribbean dishes!

The introductory question to all our participants has been "What is your favourite food?" Followed by "Why is it your favourite food? Who prepared it the first time you tasted it? When did you first prepare it yourself?" Etc....

In this edition, there are a couple of dishes, which were favourites to more than one person. I have therefore included every parent's way of preparing Ogbono and Okra Soup from Nigeria, with the addition of varying ingredients. The same goes for Peanut Butter Soup from Zimbabwe. I will encourage you to try the different methods and find one most suitable to your style. I will also like you to think of healthy ways of cooking while still enjoying the food, such as using less oil generally and cooking vegetables for as short a time as possible.

I take this opportunity to thank Mr Raymond Aaron, New York Times Top 10 Best Selling Author, my personal Coach and his team for assisting me with my book.

Please remember – if you like the aroma and taste of Scotch bonnet peppers ... have lots of drinking water nearby!

Dr Mrs Pamela Ayewoh-Bernard, MBE

(Member of the Most Excellent Order of the British Empire)

Project Team

Dr Mrs Pamela Ayewoh- Bernard, MBE: Interviewer/Compiler

Ms Asisat Lamina: Publishing Co-ordinator

Ms Jemilatu Lamina: Editorial and Template Designer

Mr John Bucknalls: Photographer

Foreword

Have you ever thought about your life purpose? You probably have not. Have you ever thought that it was time to transform your life, but never knew how? You probably have lots of things you love doing and many things you want to experience, goals you want to achieve, and you dream of an extraordinary life. Your life is filled with activities, obligations and commitments that have nothing to do with your goals or your dreams. You may be spending your life running faster and faster trying to keep up, and at the same time falling further and further away from living that extraordinary life about which you are dreaming.

When you meet someone who has transformed their life, they always seem more interesting, more engaging. They have a renewed energy; are passionate about their work, about life and in general about everything. To transform your life takes time, passion, courage and a lot of self-awareness.

Pamela is someone who has definitely overcome a life-changing event and found a way into her own transformation. When she speaks you can sense that she has turned her life around; when you read this book you will understand there is something different, something resonates, what she is saying is true, even though you may not have heard it expressed in that way before. Her vision is a world where you are doing your own thing, living your life purpose, being happy doing it and feeling extraordinary.

Pamela is reaching out to you in order to make your life better. You deserve to have the opportunity to live an extraordinary life. This book will do just that for you! It will create an extraordinary life for you. There are many recipes and suggestions in this book that you will enjoy cooking and sampling. So go for it knowing that you are changing your life for the better!

Raymond Aaron
Leading Transformational Success Mentor
New York Times Best-Selling Author

Measurements

Some common volume measures in English-speaking countries are:

Measure	Australia	Canada	UK	USA	FDA
Teaspoon	5 mL	5 ml	5 ml	4.93 ml	5 ml
Dessertspoon	10 mL		10 ml	—	—
Tablespoon	20 mL	15 ml	15 ml	14.79 ml	15 ml
Fluid ounce	—		28.41 ml	29.57 ml	30 ml
Cup	250 mL	250 ml	285 ml	236.59 ml	240 ml
Pint	568 mL†		568.26 ml	473.18 ml	—
Quart	—		1136.52 ml	946.35 ml	—
Gallon	—		4546.09 ml	3785.41 ml	—

† In South Australia, a "pint" of beer is traditionally 425 ml.

For most of the recipes, quantities are given in metric and where appropriate, measures are also given in standard cups and spoons. Standard spoon and cup measurements are level except where stated. Medium eggs should be used unless otherwise stated.

As a general rule, most of our participants have used:

1 tsp = 5ml, 1 tbsp. = 15ml, 1 cooking/kitchen spoon = 75ml, 1 cup = 250ml / 8fl. oz.

As most of our participants pointed out:

African and Caribbean-style cooking is more about feelings and taste than weighing and measuring.

MRS CAROL ALLEN

Mama Fry Stew Chicken

"Chicken pieces marinated and fried before slowly cooking in spices and BBQ sauce"

I chose to cook "Mama's fry stew chicken" because my mother, as the regular notable dish she cooked every Sunday after church, inspired it. This resonated with me because at the time church was just somewhere we went on Sundays but today it is a lifestyle choice. The first time I prepared the chicken dish was at 18 with a bit of confidence. The more I cooked it, the more my confidence grew.

When I left home, I cooked it for dinner parties and it was received very well. Now I can cook it and experiment with flavours like adding barbecue sauce, which gives the flavour of the sauce a deep rich taste that adds depth to the dish. Whenever I prepare it the memories it reminds me of is watching my father eat with such enthusiasm because he used to love his food.

INGREDIENTS
Serves 4-6
3.5kg chicken pieces
2 tbsp All-purpose seasoning
1 tbsp oregano
½ tbsp granulated garlic
1 tsp black pepper
1 tsp salt
Small green Bell pepper
Small red Bell pepper
10 fresh cherry tomatoes
1 onion
1 chilli pepper
64g Quick marinade BBQ sauce
250ml Crisp & Dry oil
4 tbsp Roast chicken gravy

1. Wash chicken pieces and arrange in oven dish
2. On top of the chicken add All-purpose seasoning oregano, garlic, black pepper and salt
3. Add red, green Bell peppers, onion and chilli pepper
4. Mix all together with your fingers
5. Add packet of BBQ sauce
6. Normally, above 5 steps can be done the day before for deep marinate
7. Pour 250ml oil into frying pan and make it very hot
8. Take off all seasoning ingredients (pepper, onions etc.) before dipping each piece of chicken into the hot oil
9. Turn chicken pieces to fry on both sides
10. After about 14 minutes, take chicken pieces out of oil and transfer to another cooking pan
11. Now add all the seasoning ingredients on top of the fried chicken pieces
12. Add 4 tbsp oil on top of the chicken to keep it moist
13. Mix Roast chicken granules with 750ml warm water and pour on the chicken pieces
14. Cover
15. Bring to the boil
16. Put lid half covered and lower the heat to simmer
17. Cook for about 35 minutes
18. Serve with Rice and peas, White rice, Brown healthy rice or Festival

Cooking time – 1 hour 15 minutes

MR EMMANUEL AMADI

Igbo Ogbono-Okra Soup with Eba

"An Igbo delicacy. Assorted meat and fish with Ogbono and Okra in a rich sauce"

This is the main food for Igbo tribe of Nigeria. My father and mother are Restaurateur in Agbor, Nigeria. The restaurant is called 'Madame Quality Restaurant". My parents had 11 children and Mum never believed in having House-help. So all the children were turned into House-help. All the children grew up knowing how to cook.

What makes a good soup is the Stock.

INGREDIENTS
Serves 2
890g chicken pieces
379g stewing beef
1 medium onion
1 tsp curry powder
1 tsp ground pepper
100ml palm oil
120g dry fish
4 tbsp ground crayfish
290g okra
1 tbsp ground Ogbono seeds
1 Knorr cube
800g garri

1. Start with the stock preparation
2. Stock mixture: ½ medium onion, ½ tsp curry powder, 1 spoonful pepper
3. Cut chicken into small pieces, put into a cooking pot and add stock mixture. Boil for 20-30 minutes until chicken pieces are soft
4. Place the chicken pieces on a tray in oven for 40 minutes at 150^0C
5. Keep the stock from the chicken
6. Put the beef pieces into a cooking pot containing 500ml water. Add stock mixture and boil for 15-20 minutes. Add beef stock to the chicken stock
7. Cut okra into small pieces, add 10ml water and blend until soft [Tip: the tip of a good okra should break easily]
8. Bring 1L stock to boil. Add 100ml palm oil, stir and taste for saltiness
9. Wash beef in 100^0C water and add to boiling mixture
10. The essence of the fish is to add flavour to the soup. Wash fish, shred to bits and remove the bones. Add to mixture, cover and bring back to the boil for approx. 2 minutes
11. Add crayfish and blended okra
12. Taste and if not happy with the taste, add more crayfish
13. Add Ogbono (if the okra is very good, you'll need less Ogbono)
14. Cook at medium heat and reduce heat near the end
15. Cover slightly for 2-3 minutes (If left covered for too long, the whole soup losses its draw and slimy nature)
16. Stir to the bottom of the pot to prevent sticking, taste and add more crayfish if needed
17. Add Knorr cube and reduce heat to very low for the last 5 minutes

Serve with Eba. Cooking time – 1 hour

Eba

1. Bring 1litre water to the boil and pour into a bowl. Sprinkle the garri on top until all the water is absorbed
2. Mash with a wooden spoon. Add 10ml water and put in the microwave [900W] for 18 seconds. Beat together

MRS MICHELLE BALACH-ALI

Fried Chicken/Fish/Rice & Irish favourite

"Being Mixed race – A Caribbean favourite with Cream mashed potatoes, cabbage and bacon"

This is a mixture of Grenadian and Irish cooking. My Nan taught me how to prepare Irish food while my Mum taught me how to prepare Caribbean food.

My children love this dish because it is tasty and it has bits of everything. My dad use to grow thyme in the garden, so he puts thyme on everything and that is what I now do. Every time I prepare this dish I think of my Mum's cooking – I think she is the best cook in the world!

In order to make this my favourite dish, I've had to try different ingredients until I got what I finally liked.

INGREDIENTS

Serves 6

8 medium size potatoes	10 pieces Fish – seabass
½ medium size cabbage	15g thyme
340g red cabbage	172g onions
424g Easy cook rice	254g red pepper
2kg chicken pieces	170g green pepper
100ml Maggi Liq. Seasoning	280g spring onion
Black pepper	3 tbsp butter
1 tbsp All pepper seasoning	167g red onions
3 tbsp garlic	352g diced tomatoes
1 Scotch bonnet pepper	lemon, milk
1 tbsp dry chilli	5 bacon rashers
424g flour	160g sweet corn
250ml vegetable oil	500g green beans
	240g red kidney beans

1. Peel potatoes, put in pot and cover with extra inch of water above them
2. Remove outside layer of cabbage, shred, wash, put in pot and cover with water half an inch above them
3. Red cabbage – shred, put in pot with water half an inch above. Cook for 20-30 minutes
4. Rice – into pot and cover with water, 3ins above level of rice. Bring to boil and simmer for 20 minutes. Wash with cold water and leave to drain. Mop with kitchen paper towel
5. Chicken pieces - add Black pepper, All pepper seasoning and garlic and leave to marinate for 2 hours
6. Then add thyme, diced scotch bonnet and mix thoroughly. Add chilli and mix thoroughly
7. Put oil into frying pan and warm up
8. Coat each piece of chicken with flour (not too much flour) and put into the very hot oil
9. Chicken breasts in first as they cook quickly, followed by the thighs. Fry for 10 minutes turning once until both sides are golden brown
10. Similarly, coat the pieces of fish and fry in the hot oil
11. The Irish Connection:
12. Once the potatoes are cooked, drain and dry away the water under low heat – to make it fluffy
13. Add butter and 1 tbsp. milk. Mix thoroughly with masher. Add 1 tsp onions and spring onions. Put into a large bowl and garnish with more spring onions and thyme
14. Check the white cabbage, drain, cut into small pieces in the pot with a large knife. Add 2 tbsp butter, spring onions and put into a large bowl
15. Do the same with the red cabbage and add it to the white cabbage when it is cold
16. Grill the bacon, cut into small pieces with a pair of scissors and add to the cabbage mixture [1 side dish]
17. Add 56ml oil to frying pan and make boiling hot
18. Add dice tomatoes, dice spring onions, 2 tbsp garlic and fry mixture for 10 minutes. Deseed red pepper, cut into long strands and dice, deseed green pepper and cut into cubes
19. Add Maggi seasoning, 1 tsp black pepper and mixed red/green pepper. Stir continuously
20. Add sweet corn, red kidney beans, spring onions and frozen green beans
21. Mix thoroughly and fry for another 8 minutes for the beans to defrost and still be crispy.
22. Taste. Add 1 tbsp sugar
23. Add to layer of rice and mix
24. Cut lemon and add to the chicken to garnish. Cucumber to garnish

MRS FOLASHADE BAMGBALA

Grandma's Memory Pancake

"A mixture of flour and sugar fried in oil"

I have chosen this foreign diet because it reminds me of my childhood with my aunties and uncles. It brings back memories of my Grandma sitting there in her chair. She died just four years ago at the age of 96 years.

This is a Sunday sort of meal. We always used to look forward to Sundays. My granny 'bless her' always did the batter in a big bowl with no special measurements used. She used to put a big portion in the griddle and we all queue for our turn. We loved the pancake so much that we talked about it all the time.

Nobody can make pancakes like my Grandma!

INGREDIENTS
Serves 2
100g plain flour
2 tbsp of sugar
¼ tsp of salt
1 large egg
250ml milk + water or plain water
5ml oil

1. Mix all the dry ingredients – flour, sugar and salt

2. Break the egg into the milk. Beat/whisk until smooth

3. Add slowly to the dry ingredients

4. Mix until smooth [You can add more milk/water if watery consistent is required]

5. You can put in the fridge at this stage of complete mixture or fry straight away.

6. Add tablespoon of oil to a frying pan

7. Pour mixture into the frying pan to give an even layer over the pan

8. Fry over medium heat until brown on one side

9. Toss or gently turn over with a flat spoon

10. Fry the side until brown

Serve with sugar sprinkled on top

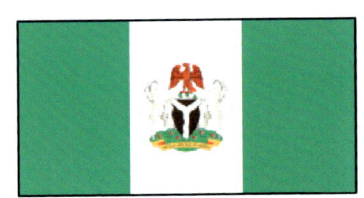
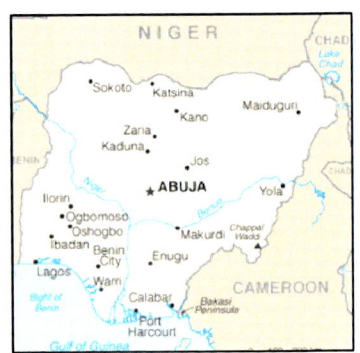

MRS JULLIETTE ABIA DICKSON

Afang/Ugu and Edikaikong Soup

"Green vegetables with assorted meat and fish soup from Calabar Nigeria"

This is made up of green vegetables, which are good for you when not over cooked, and it tastes good. For health reasons, I use very little oil in my cooking.

My Mum cooked this for me back home when I was young. I was always in the kitchen watching her cooking and I just learnt it from her. At age 14, I could cook it myself. Now, I cook it about three times a month. It brings back memories of cooking together with Mum back home in Nigeria especially since Mum passed away when I was 16 years old.

I should be eating this more often because it is good for me!

INGREDIENTS
Serves a large family
1kg Assorted meat: Cow's foot, tripe, beef, chicken, fish and prawns
150ml Stock from meat
3 tbsp palm oil
1 diced medium size onion
500g dry fish
2 tbsp ground crayfish
Salt – to taste
Pepper – to taste
1 Scotch bonnet pepper
600g ground Okazi leaves
300g shredded Spinach
300g Ugu leaves (fluted pumpkin leaves)
Cassava – African salad strands
Pounded yam

1. Assorted meat cut into medium size pieces, clean and boil with just enough water to cover the meat
2. Drain to get excess meat fat out for a more healthy meal. Keep some stock for cooking
3. Into a pot put the meat (1kg) with 150ml of meat stock, add 250ml water and all the ingredients with Okazi leaves, 3 tbsp palm oil and boil for 10 minutes
4. Wash leaves and add the spinach and Ugu leaves. Stir and taste
5. Add more water – 250ml. Cover and let it simmer for 20 minutes.
6. Remove from heat and let it cool down
7. Serve with Pounded yam or Eba

> **INGREDIENTS**
> *Serves a large family*
> *For White Soup*
> Okra - handful
> 2 tbsp crayfish
> Utazi leaves- handful
> 3 tbsp ground prawns
> Ground pepper – to taste
> Salt – to taste
> 500g dry fish
> Garlic/ginger
> 2 Maggi cubes
> 2 tbsp Yam powder (thickener)

1. Similar preparation to above. It is called White soup because white pounded yam flour is used to thicken it
2. 150ml meat stock in pot, add ingredients and 500ml water
3. Boil for 5-10 minutes
4. Wash Utazi (Bitter) leaves with hot water. Add 1 tbsp wet leaves to the cooking pot
5. Add 1kg boiled assorted meat cut into medium size pieces. Stir

6. Soup is cooked when colour changes, it's bubbling and consistence thickness
7. Serve with Pounded yam

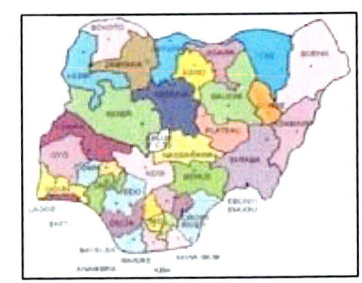

MRS ADERONKE FADAYIRO

Yam and Liver Stew

"Fried liver in a spicy sauce"

This was usually our Sunday breakfast when we were growing up. My Mum taught me how to cook it. Now I cook it for my husband and daughter and they love it.

It brings back fond memories of my Mum whenever I eat it. My Mum was a very good mother and a good cook. Now, apart from cooking it for my family, I make it as a special treat for special guests to our house.

INGREDIENTS
Serves 4
500g Liver
250ml oil
1 medium onion
10g crayfish (optional)
30g smoked prawns
5g red scotch bonnet pepper
400g tin tomatoes
2 Knorr tubes
½ tsp curry powder
½ tsp ground ginger powder
½ tsp mixed herbs or thyme
2½ tsp salt
8 slices of Yam
3 tsp sugar
50g washed spinach

1. Wash liver pieces, cut into smaller pieces and put into blender
2. Pulse blend – 3 times to have small chunks/pieces of liver
3. Put into cooking pot and pour in 100ml cooking oil
4. Stir under high heat
5. Fry liver for about 10 minutes stirring continuously until brown, making sure there are no lumps of liver
6. Add salt (optional)
7. Add 3 slices of onions, put remaining onions into blender
8. Add tomatoes and pepper to blender and blend to a smooth paste
9. Add to pan of liver
10. Add Knorr cubes, salt to taste and stir to avoid liver sticking to bottom of pot
11. Add curry powder, mixed herbs/thyme and ginger powder
12. Wash prawns (can cut large pieces into smaller bits) and add to liver
13. Add crayfish
14. Add 150ml cooking oil
15. Cover and reduce heat
16. Simmer until liver is properly fried - 20 minutes stirring occasionally
17. Meanwhile, cut the yam into 8 thick slices, peel and wash
18. Put into 1L water in a pot
19. Add teaspoon salt and sugar and bring to the boil until yam is soft – approx. 10 minutes
20. Wash spinach, shred into small pieces, add to liver stew and stir
21. Turn off heat immediately (1 minute)
(Save time by starting with the yam and cook the stew while the yam is boiling)

Approximate cooking time: 30 minutes

Larok Food Express
For delicious home cooked Nigerian meals
ronkefadayiro@gmail.com
+44 (0)1234 343189/ (0)7886089451

MRS PAULINE GARRIQUES

"Dutty Girl"

"Tin mackerel in tomato sauce with breadfruit"

I like this dish because it is easy to prepare. It takes a short time in the kitchen. This is a favourite for every-one particularly for men.

It reminds me of back home, my childhood and my father in the fields working.
Happy times
Really …..

INGREDIENTS
Serves 4
1 tbsp Coconut oil
1 medium size Shallots (form of onions)
Garlic
1 tomato – medium size
Spring onion
1 Scotch bonnet pepper
Pimento
400g Pilchards in tomato sauce
Fresh thyme
¼ tsp black pepper
1kg Breadfruit

1. Put 1 tbsp coconut oil in pot, add shallots
2. Add shallots, garlic, fresh tomatoes, stir and fry until onions and tomatoes are slightly cooked ~ 5 minutes
3. Optional – Add 2 slices of scotch pepper without the seeds
4. Add 10 seeds of pimento; Cook under low heat, cover and simmer for approx. 5 minutes
5. Tin of Pilchards = Dutty Girl
6. Add Pilchards and one stem of spring onion to the pot
7. Rinse fresh thyme and add 4 sprigs of thyme and black pepper
8. Simmer for 5 minutes
9. Prepare Breadfruit in advance
10. Roast in open fire or stove under high heat until skin goes burnt a little
11. In summer – can put on Barbeque grill to roast. This gives it a smoky flavour inside
12. Leave in oven for 1 hour at 175^0C
13. To check if it is cooked, stick a knife in the middle a CLEAR knife means it is cooked
14. Bring out of oven and cool for about 10 minutes
15. Cut into slices after removing the "heart" to discard
16. Peel off the skin and cut further into very thin slices – 4 slices suitable for each person
17. If eating the breadfruit later, it can be warmed in the microwave – 1 minute at high heat
18. Serve with Avogadro pear to garnish

Approximate cooking time: 15 minutes when breadfruit is prepared in advance

MRS CHARMAINE GONERA

Mupunga Une Dovi Ne Huku

"Rice in peanut butter with chicken and green vegetables"

My grandmother Gogo Margreth Chidemo who used to live in Murehwa village in Zimbabwe used to make this lovely dish every time we went to visit her whilst on holidays. This was our welcome meal. She would ask me to find a chicken running around in her yard and it would be slaughtered and cooked by her. She used to grow rice on her own field – proper organic rice which was cooked in a clay pot. When she came from the village to the city to visit us, she used to bring a live chicken and rice.

I was 8 years old when I first ate it. I used to watch my grandmother cooking it and from the age of 12, I started learning how to cook it. Now when I cook here, it takes me back and reminds me of my grandmother who is now dead. At first, my children thought it was odd eating rice with peanut butter. So one day, I cooked it and rolled the rice into round shapes like a ball. They loved it!

Now, my children like it as rice balls and they ask, "When are we having rice balls?"

INGREDIENTS
Serves 5
1.5kg Boiling chicken
1 kg Thai rice
12 tsp Peanut butter
400g chopped tomatoes
2 Maggi cubes
1 tbsp Royco usavi mix chicken seasoning
1 tsp ginger/garlic paste
1 medium size onion
3 tsp Olive oil
1 tsp salt (or to taste)
400g spring green vegetables
½ tsp All-purpose seasoning

1. Wash chicken pieces, transfer to pot with 900ml water
2. Add All purpose seasoning, Maggi cubes, ginger and garlic paste and cover
3. Bring to boil for about 1 hour until only the oil from the chicken is left
4. Add onions and fry for 5 minutes
5. Add tomatoes and fry until tomatoes have disintegrated and become sauce – 10 minutes
6. Keep mixing and stirring
7. Take 300ml of water to rinse tomato can, add chicken mix and add to sauce
8. Cover and simmer under low heat for 10 minutes
9. Taste for saltiness
10. If watery, add 1 tsp gravy granules to thicken it. Simmer for another 10 minute
11. Meanwhile, wash rice and put in a pot
12. Boil 1L water and add to the rice
13. Add 1 tsp salt and boil for about 45 minutes until rice is light and fluffy
14. Rice has to be over cooked
15. Add 12 tsp of peanut butter
16. Mix thoroughly with a wooden spoon for 15 minutes
17. Cover under low heat for 10 minutes
18. Mix again until you get a paste-like mixture
19. Vegetables: Cut off stem and chop into thin slices
20. Put 3 tsp oil into pot and warm it up
21. Add 1 vegetable cube (or salt) to melt in the oil
22. Pour in the vegetables and fry under medium heat for about 10 minutes
23. Taste and see that the vegetables are not crunchy and are cooked

Cooking time – 2 hours

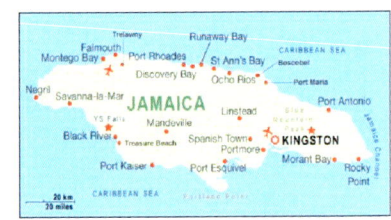

MRS WEMA GRANT

Caribbean Fried Snapper

"Marinated fried fish served with salad"

This dish reminds me of going for a picnic and packing a picnic lunch. I left Jamaica when I was 19 years old and by then I could cook. My Stepmother taught me how to cook. We had a large family so I had to learn how to cook early. We do not eat it much now but with fishes that have lots of bones, it is best to fry them so the bones can be easily crushed.

This dish is special because a lot of ingredients are used for it. I eat much more of English food now rather than Caribbean food because I have been here for a long time. So preparing a Caribbean dish becomes really different.

INGREDIENTS
Serves 3
3x 285g Fish snappers
550g Sweet potatoes
Ground Black pepper
Coarse Black pepper
Lamb seasoning (instead of fish seasoning)
Garlic – whole glove
Cayenne pepper
Caribbean Everyday seasoning
Parsley
500ml vegetable oil
2 medium red/green Bell peppers
2 red onions – medium size
540g Cou-cou   2 fresh tomatoes
Baby lettuce, cucumber, baby plum tomatoes
Malt vinegar, Baillon powder, Mayolia

1. Night before: Wash, clean fishes and cover with salt. In morning, rinse off salt in the hope that some salt would have been absorbed by the fish
2. Wash sweet potato and put in oven, Gas mark 6 for 1½ hours
3. Prepare a mixture of: ½ tsp Black pepper, 4 Garlic gloves cut into thin slices, ½ tsp Lamb seasoning, ½ tsp Cayenne pepper, ½ tsp Parsley and ½ tsp Everyday seasoning. Add 4 serving spoon of plain flour to the mixture
4. This can be prepared up to few hours before use
5. Add 1 red onion chopped into cubes, 1 tbsp lamb seasoning and 2 tsp turmeric for colour
6. Put 500ml oil into frying pan, make oil very hot
7. Make sure fish is thoroughly dry by blotting with towel
8. Put generous amount of seasoning mixture inside and on outside of fish adding more Black pepper to the diagonal slits on the outside
9. Put gently into frying oil
10. Fry on one side for approx. 15 minutes under low heat. Turn over and fry the other side
11. Meanwhile, wash Cou-cou, cut off ends and cut into thin slices
12. Cut 2nd onion into medium size slices, same as the deseeded red and green peppers
13. After frying the fishes, put the Cou-cou into the same frying oil, add the cut onion and fry until golden brown and dry (not burnt)
14. Turn over the Cou-cou and take all out within 10 minutes. Then fry the cut red/green peppers
15. Salad: Baby lettuce, whole cucumber, Baby plum tomatoes, 2 medium tomatoes cut into wedges
16. Wash lettuce and put in drainer to get rid of excess water
17. Take cucumber, wash and scratch it straight down with a fork to create a pattern. Slice sideways to give a nice design
18. Wash baby plum tomatoes and fry them for about 1 minute
19. Put fishes on top of Cou-cou, garnish with fried onions, peppers and tomatoes
20. Sprinkle with Malt vinegar to cut down the grease
21. Sprinkle with sweet vegetable Baillon powder and serve with the salad and sweet potato
22. Sprinkle Mayolia – vegetarian mayonnaise as a dressing on the salad

MS IMADE IDEHEN

Banga Soup

"Sea food delicacy with chicken, snails, turkey and eaten with Fufu"

I like this food because my Mum used to make it when special guests were expected at the house. A special meal for important people.

I watched my Mum cooking it as a child. Now, when I want to show people where I am from, I prepare this dish. I prepare it when male guests are visiting the house for the first time especially if they are Itsekiri people. In wedding ceremonies, even though there's rice banga soup must be prepared for the top important guests.

Mum has passed away and my only inheritance was a set of cooking pots. So whenever I prepare this dish, I think of sweet memories of my Mum and her cooking. Sweet, sweet memories……….

INGREDIENTS
Serves 5

1kg chicken boiler
257g onions 2 med
Knorr chicken cubes
140g smoked turkey   313g fresh tomatoes
115g snails   74g okra
398g fresh fish (descaled Tilapia)   Scent leaves
536g crab   12g Uda long black seeds (photo)
350g smoked fish   Small seeds (photo)
40g scotch bonnet pepper x3   Aizuza leaves
214g red Bell pepper x2   174g lime x2
180g fresh prawns   Ground crayfish
400g Trofai palmnut concentrate   Ghanaian Fufu

1. Chicken pieces: wash and clean with hot water, remove all attached hair and put in a pot. Add whole sliced onion, 1 cube seasoning stock, 200ml water and cover to boil
2. Snails: clean and cut into two, wash with alum/lime to remove the slime around the snails. Rinse with tap water
3. Prawns: wash, remove outer shell and black thin vessel in middle of the prawns. Add hot water for few minutes and rinse with warm water
4. Crab: remove the legs, prize open with knife, clean the piece and legs with lime and rinse with warm water. Keep only the big legs. Pour hot water on all the pieces and rinse with warm water. Add the crabs and snails to the chicken in the cooking pot. Add 400ml water, stir and cover
5. Smoked turkey: Already half-cooked. Wash with hot water
6. Blend: Add many peppers to prevent "throw up" due to the seafood ingredients. Burn Udu in a naked flame and put in blender, add Bell pepper, scotch bonnet pepper, tomatoes, 1 tsp seeds, 1 tsp small seeds, 1 whole onion, 200ml water and 3 tsp crayfish. Blend
7. Add mixture to pot of meat. Rinse blender with 20ml water and add to pot
8. Add whole can of palm oil, add prawns, 5 minutes later add 1 tsp scent leaves. Stir and cover
9. Wash smoked fish, remove its bones, pour boiled water and rinse out. Add into pot in large bits
10. Add smoked turkey, 2 chicken stock cubes, salt to taste (1/4 tsp) and ½ cover pot under medium heat
11. Wash okra, cut off top and bottom, slice down middle and cut into big chunks
12. Fresh fish: clean out fish, rub and clean with lime. Rinse with hot water for few minutes. Rinse with cold water – twice and coat with a thin layer of salt (<1/4 tsp and done earlier). Add to pot. Cook for only 10 minutes. Add okra
13. Leave open and stir gently
14. Serve with Fufu
15. Start with 500ml water
16. Add 200g Fufu and stir. Put on fire stirring until it goes hard and cooked

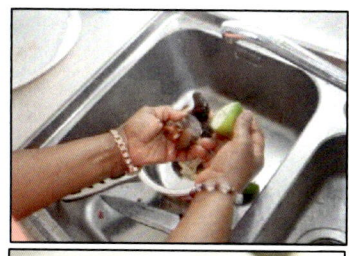

This is an expensive dish because of the ingredients
Cooking time one hour

 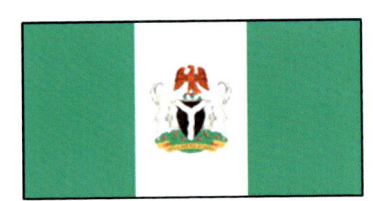 

CHIEF MATTHEW OSAGHE IRIA (JP)

Esan Ogbono Soup with Pounded Yam

"Draw soup – assorted meat and fish in a rich aroma sauce"

My Mum taught me how to cook this food. She is from South-East Esan land and the area produces 50% of Edo State production of Ogbono seeds. While growing up in Ebelle town, I used to watch my Mum do all the cooking and then I learnt from her how to cook my now favourite soup. As a bachelor, I was able to cook both Nigerian and English dishes and my friends used to come to my house to eat. My work colleagues loved my jollof and fried rice and I used to take extra packed lunches to work to give them. One of them was so impressed with my culinary skills that he asked me to prepare food for his son's birthday party. I prepared two coolers worth of jollof and fried rice. My friends have always said that I should have been a Chef!

When I got married, I taught my wife how to cook it and she became the best cook for Ogbono soup in that part of Lagos. Ogbono soup is also known as Draw soup and because of its nutritional value and mobile friendliness, you will like to eat more and more ....

INGREDIENTS
Serves 4-6
120g catfish
210g meat
315g chicken
1½ tsp thyme
3 tsp All-purpose seasoning
1½ tsp curry powder
¼ tsp of salt
100ml palm oil
95g Ogbono seed

90g okra
55g spinach
40g onions
2 Maggi cubes
½ tsp pepper
275g poundo iyan powder
1 tsp olive oil

1. Add fish to 30ml water and boil for 10 minutes
2. Add cut pieces of meat to 20ml water, ½ tsp curry powder, ½ tsp thyme, 1tsp All-purpose seasoning, onion, salt, ¼ tsp pepper, 1 Maggi cube cover and boil for 15 minutes
   Add cut pieces of chicken to 30ml water, 1 tsp curry powder, 1 tsp thyme, 2 tsp All-purpose seasoning, ¼ tsp pepper, 1 Maggi cube and boil for 15 minutes
3. Remove chicken pieces and put in oven at 250^0C for 30 minutes, keep the stock
4. Grind the Ogbono in a blender until smooth as very fine powder
5. Remove beef meat from pot and add the stock to the chicken stock
6. Soup: Take a dry cooking pot and put on high heat to make it hot
7. Add 2 cooking spoons of palm oil
8. Add the Ogbono and stir to have a paste and remove from heat
9. Chop the spinach, remove stump end of okra and chop into small pieces
10. Add 5ml of water to okra and blend for 20 seconds
11. Rinse fish with cold water
12. Add 650ml of chicken/meat mixed stock to the Ogbono paste and bring back to the cooker
13. Cook under high heat for 2 minutes
14. Reduce to medium heat while stirring and then to low heat
15. Leave the pot open
16. Stir and whisk at the same time and within 5 minutes
17. Add fish, beef, chicken and okra
18. Stir for 1 minute right to bottom of pot to prevent sticking
19. Add spinach and taste for saltiness. Stir and serve out

Pounded Yam

1. 110ml cold water into pot and boil
2. Add poundo iyan powder to water
3. Add olive oil
4. Stir sternly and vigorously
5. Turn until smooth paste
6. Add water to required consistency

MRS HANNAH ABIMBOLA JOLAOSO

Egusi Soup with Pounded Yam

"A delicious combination of Egusi seeds in palm oil based soup with assorted meat and spinach"

This is my favourite food and a dish that my Mum made regularly when I was young and we the children loved it. She did not let us cook it ourselves so we learnt by watching her. She cooks hers in a slightly different way to mine. The love of coming home from school or university and looking forward to Egusi soup and pounded yam!

Since I started cooking it, my friends always ask, "how do you cook that?" They loved it!! I cooked it for the first time when I was at university and stayed with my uncle. His wife was away so I had to cook for his family. They liked it!!!

INGREDIENTS
Serves 4-6

- 100g smoked catfish fillet
- 400g tinned plum tomatoes
- 166g Onions x2
- 1 large red Bell pepper
- 1 scotch bonnet pepper
- 7 tsp Palm oil
- 1 tsp Jumbo chicken stock
- Assorted meat:
- Tripe
- Cow's skin
- Beef
- Crayfish
- Dry garlic
- Dried ginger
- Thyme
- Salt to taste
- Curry powder
- 275g Egusi seeds
- 275g Yam powder
- 4x160g bundles of Spinach

1. Soak Catfish in hot water and cover with water to about 1 inch above the Catfish for 10 minutes
2. Boil meat: Assorted meat, add 2 onions, 1 tsp curry powder, 1 tbsp thyme, 1 tsp dry garlic, 1 tsp dried ginger and 2 tbsp salt. 30 minutes for Beef and one hour for tripe and cow's skin
3. Blend: Tomatoes, 1 large onion, Bell pepper and scotch pepper
4. Put empty pot on fire. Add 7 tbsp palm oil. Warm for 1 minute
5. Add blended mixture, 1 tsp salt, 1 heaped tsp Jumbo stock, 3 tsp ground crayfish, 200ml meat stock and cook for approximately 20 minutes under medium heat. Stir and taste for salt
6. Egusi: Wash seeds at least twice. Put in blender; add 1 onion and 300ml water. Blend to still see the grains - not too smooth
7. Frying: Put 6 tbsp palm oil in a pot on fire so the oil melts but not smoky
8. Pour in the blended Egusi, stir and fry – making sure the Egusi does not stick to the bottom of the pot. Cook until water has dried from the mixture
9. Rinse Catfish fillet with water and add to blended tomato stew
10. After 25 minutes of blended tomato stew, add the fried Egusi
11. Cut meat into small pieces and add to the pot
12. Spinach: Chop into small pieces, wash and rinse under running water in a sieve. Add boiled water to a container of the leaves covering the leaves for 2-3 minutes. Strain off the water, press down with a spoon to make sure most of the water has drained off. Add to cooking pot, cover under low heat for 5 minutes and food is ready

Pounded Yam

1. Boil water and put 1L into a pot
2. Add pounded yam powder, add 100ml water, turn, cover under low heat for 5 minutes. Beat and stir until mixture is nice, smooth and soft.

www.hannahj.co.uk

MRS DEBORAH JOSEPH-EDOYIBO

African Salad & Owerri Vegetable Soup

"Ugba and Abacha African salad as appetizer followed by stock fish, catfish, cocoyam and assorted vegetable leaves in a rich soup"

This is my favourite soup and I grew up eating this soup regularly. I taught myself how to prepare it by watching my Mum cooking it back home in Nigeria. I also watched Mum cooking rice, plantain and stew but I was not allowed to cook. She felt I was not as good as she was. I first prepared it when a friend asked me to in Nigeria when I had left home.

Every time I prepare it here, it reminds me of back home when I was growing up. This was the main soup in Owerri. Now, my husband and I enjoy eating this at home.

INGREDIENTS
Serves 4-6

556g Stock fish
24g dried prawns
38g onions
25g Crayfish
Palm oil
Salt
190g Ugba (Oil bean)
2 tsp Pepper
120g Abacha (made from cassava)
1 Knorr Aromatic-all purpose-seasoning
330g Cocoyam
80g smoked Catfish fillet
10g Ogiri
8g Dry Okazzi leaves
103g Oha leaves
Dried fish
274g Ugu (pumpkin) leaves
Uzazi

1. Prior to start, boil Stock fish for 1½ hours
2. For Salad: Slice and dice the onion and wash 12g dried prawns. Put into a mortar
3. Add 20g crayfish and pound mixture in the mortar. Add a pinch of diced onions and grind to a very fine paste
4. Put an empty cooking pot onto the fire
5. Add 1½ tbsp. of palm oil, ½ tsp salt, diced onions and the mashed paste from the mortar
6. Fry for one minute
7. Add Ugba, pepper, 146g stockfish (hand shredded into small pieces) and Abacha. Stir. Fry for about 5 minutes
8. Add Knorr stock cube for taste. Serve with Palm wine
9. You can add potash if you have it, but start with the potash in the red oil before adding the other ingredients. Owerri people use only Ugba and stock fish
10. Owerri Soup: Peel Cocoyam, wash, cut and put into a pot. Add 1500ml stock from the Stock fish and bring to boil
11. Meanwhile put the Catfish into a bowl and add 1 tsp salt, wash and rinse with warm water
12. Put 12g dried prawns into the mortar, wash 5g crayfish, and add to mortar. Pound to a fine paste
13. After 10 minutes of boiling (Step 12) add 5tsp palm oil, Catfish, 2 tsp shredded pepper, pounded paste of crayfish and prawns. Add 2 tsp salt to taste, shred the Stock fish and add to pot
14. After 15 minutes of boiling, bring out Cocoyam and put into the mortar and pound
15. Ogiri is African Maggi cube. Mix one cube with 1 tsp hot water and put into cooking pot
16. Wash Okazzi with hot water to soften it and add to pot (Most important leaf to have in the soup)
17. Allow to boil, then simmer
18. Add Oha leaves – tearing the leaves with your hands
19. Next is Ugu leaves – cut into small pieces with a small knife
20. Once Ugu leaves are added, bring to boil and after 1 minute the Soup is ready

MRS SISSI LUNGWA

Fumbua

"A rich vegetable dish with peanut butter and fish"

Fumbua is my favourite dish. My Mum taught me how to prepare the dish. It is a dish from my Mum's tribe and it was her favourite food so she taught all her children how to prepare it. Fortunately, I married a man whose Mum used to cook it for him as well. So, it is now OUR favourite dish in my present family.

Whenever I cook it, it reminds me of home, my Mum and grandma who also loves it as her favourite food. Thinking back now, I didn't like it when Mum used to get my sister and I to cook on Saturdays and Sundays but when I got married and found out that it was my husband's favourite food as well, I was glad I learnt how to cook it!!

INGREDIENTS
Serves 4
250g Fumbia vegetable
Spring onion x3
1 medium onion
1 tsp garlic
Palm oil
2 tbsp tomato paste
1 green scotch bonnet pepper
3 Maggi cubes
200g chopped tomatoes
500g smooth peanut butter
Salt
50g Dry Congolese fish

1. Previously: Soak the fish in hot water for 24 hours (from day before)
2. Wash vegetable in a large bowl with cold water
3. Remove vegetable from bowl making sure all debris is left behind in the water especially if it is fresh vegetable from the market. Do this 3x
4. Put 1L boiling water into a pot and put in the vegetable
5. Add spring onion, garlic, sprinkle 2 Maggi cubes on top
6. Add 3 tbsp palm oil, cover and boil for 20 minutes under high heat
7. Add tomato paste, tomato puree, peanut butter and last of Maggi cube
8. Remove fish from water, remove all bones and shred into small pieces, add to cooking pot
9. Add ½ tsp salt
10. DO NOT STIR, DO NOT TURN
11. Cover and simmer for another 10 minutes for the peanut butter to cook
12. After 10 minutes, stir and turn, taste for saltiness
13. It's ready
14. Used Salt fish and Kwanga (sliced cassava) as side plates

Serve with any meat or fish dish

Cooking time – 45 minutes

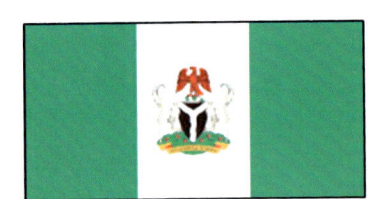

MRS LILIAN MARTINS

Ayamase

"Called Designer Stew or Green Dynamite – green peppers with assorted meat in a spicy sauce"

For the older women – the generation before us, this was a delicacy prepared to get back your husband after a quarrel. In this age, it has turned out to be a delicacy at parties but meant for dignitaries at the high table. It is meant to be eaten on leaves with rice.

I first ate it at a party. My son went to a Nigerian restaurant, ate it and came to tell me he has just had a most delicious meal. It so happened that I knew the owner of the restaurant and she told me it was Ayamase. My son kept going to the restaurant, so I decided to start cooking it at home for him.

I have added my own special skills to it so it tastes better than any-body else's.

From Yorubaland.

INGREDIENTS
Serves 5-6

1.2kg of meat:

Tripe	187g x6 green Bell pepper
Kidney	29 sticks hot chilli pepper
Cow's foot	18 Scotch bonnet pepper
Cow's skin	390g Basmati premium rice
Goat meat	500ml palm oil
Turkey meat	5 Maggi crayfish
7½ medium onions	50g Locust beans
Salt	4 medium eggs

1. Wash assorted meat and put into pot, peel onions and slice into pot
2. Add 3 tsp salt, cover and boil with the water from the meat
3. Wash eggs and put in the same pot of meat
4. After 7 minutes take out eggs, peel with a toothpick in order for the eggs to absorb the stew later
5. Put in blender:
6. Deseeded green peppers, 6 onions (reduces the spiciness), scotch bonnet pepper, chilli pepper sticks
7. Blend but not smooth
8. Drain to remove excess water added for blending. Keep drained water
9. Rice: Rinse 4-5 times to get rid of the starch until water gets clear
10. Add 1L water and bring to the boil covered
11. Once boiled, rinse again until the water is clear. Add enough water to about an inch above the rice. Cover and cook under low heat. 20 minutes total cooking time
12. Put 350ml palm oil into a big pot – the palm oil heats up until it is bleached for this dish
13. Add a slice of onion which will show when to add the blended mixture by changing colour
14. Once the onion slice turns dark brown or black (about 25 minutes) take the pot off the fire
15. Add the blended mixture. Bring to boil and cover for about 20 minutes
16. Add eggs, stir, cover and boil for another 10 minutes
17. Crumble in Maggi crayfish cubes
18. Add Locust beans and stir
19. Add 2 kitchen spoonful of blended pepper water
20. After 5 minute boiling time add meat
21. Meat boiled for 1 hour for cow's foot and skin. Others boiled for 45 minutes

Can be served with additional dodo or moi-moi. Cooking time – 1.5 hours

LOLA MK

Yoruba Okra Soup

"Yoruba style Okra soup with assorted meat, fish and mushroom"

This is my favourite soup for two reasons; first, it is very easy and quick to make and secondly it is nutritious. It can actually be used as a drink by itself without the Eba and Ground rice to go with it. The meat, fish and mushrooms are cut to small pieces and are easy to swallow even for children.

My grand "Mama" first prepared this for me when I was about 7 years old. While she is preparing it, you could hear the pounding of the yam going on in the background. I was allowed to start preparing it when I was about 11 years old so that by the time I came to the UK at age 12 I could prepare it very well.

When I prepare it now, it is a way for me to connect with my roots. I try not to westernise it as it helps me to remember my village and grand Mama. It really connects me to home and for my child to appreciate food from where I originated.

INGREDIENTS
Serves 5
Assorted meat:
7g tripe
12g beef   Chilli pepper
7g gizzard   1 tsp bitter leaf
9g liver   2 Knorr soup seasoning mix
2 scotch bonnet pepper   2 medium onions
1 Jumbo cube   4 tbsp Palm oil
Salt   50g Bonga fillets (Dry fish)
50g Stock fish fillet   50g smoked whole Mackerel
Iru (Locust beans)   100g mushroom
2 tsp ground crayfish   250g Okra
1 tsp raw crayfish   50g smoked catfish

1. Wash meat with warm water and put all in one pot
2. Add scotch bonnet pepper, Jumbo cube and salt
3. Cover and boil for 25 minutes
4. Put 600ml warm water into a cooking pot
5. Add Stock fish, Catfish and Iru
6. Blend ground crayfish, raw crayfish and pepper and add to the pot
7. Add Bitter leaves, cover and cook for 2 minutes
8. Add Knorr soup seasoning mix and palm oil
9. Cover and cook for 8 minutes
10. Add meat
11. Wash mushroom and cut into pieces and add to pot
12. Wash okra, cut into medium size pieces but do not blend. Add to pot with one cup of water
13. Cut and debone whole Mackerel into large pieces and add to pot with other fishes
14. Cover and cook for 5 minutes

Served with Eba, Pounded yam or Semolina
Cooking time – 1 hour

MRS MARYAM MUAZU

Suya/Tsire

"Authentic Hausa home cooked - marinated and oven grilled Beef, Lamb, Chicken and Goat meat served with fresh tomatoes and salad"

This is used as an appetiser. I like Suya because of its taste and all my family love it. We eat it mostly at weekends and when we have visitors. It is so popular within the family that I decided to start cooking it as a business from home.

Nobody taught me as such, I watched people cooking it back home in Nigeria and since I have been here, I have made up my own ingredients and mixtures, which everybody likes. Whenever we eat it here, it reminds me of home in Nigeria and it is nice that my whole family here like Suya.

INGREDIENTS
Serves one family
6kg Assorted meat:
Beef
Lamb
Chicken
Goat
Kuli kuli
8g ginger
2g garlic
3 medium onions
3.5g scotch bonnet pepper
Yaji

1. Make sure all meat bought are fresh and lean – all fat must be removed
2. Cut meat into thin slices
3. Prepare seasoning
4. Kuli kuli – by product when groundnut is fried and the oil squeezed out of it
5. Blend ginger, garlic, onion and scotch bonnet pepper without water. Use groundnut oil instead
6. Rub blended mixture round meat slices
7. Rub small amount of Kuli kuli round meat slices
8. Put in oven at 240^0C for 1hour 30 minutes.
9. Turn meat over and leave for another 30 minutes
10. Do second turning of meat and bake for another 15 minutes
11. Take out of oven and serve with tomatoes and salad
12. For Barbeque instead of using an oven:
13. Cut lean beef
14. String the meat onto skewers
15. Rub blended mixture round the meat
16. Rub Kuli kuli
17. Put on barbeque rack

Cooking time – approximately 3 hours

ZARASH – Authentic Hausa Home Cooked Food
+44 (0)7404708444

 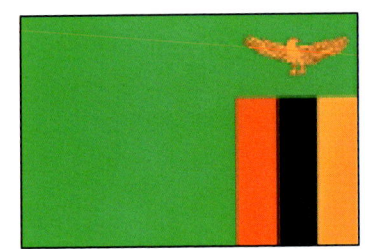 

MRS GETRUDE CHULU NYONI

Zambia Family Meal

"An earthy family feast with kapenta, okra, ground peanut and vegetables"

This is the main traditional food in most parts of Zambia. I grew up eating it and became so beautiful... I crave for it. If I have not eaten it for a week, I feel homesick.

My mother taught me how to cook it when I was about 10 years old. My grandmother taught me how to prepare the groundnuts ones. They taught me other dishes as well but this one is my favourite and I can easily get the ingredients here.

This meal brings back memories of sitting down to eat properly. When guests of my background come to visit, they feel very welcome and feel at home when served this meal. I have taught my children to sit down to eat this as a traditional meal and have taught the girls how to prepare it but they are still learning…

INGREDIENTS
Serves 6
1 medium cabbage
3 medium onions
300g kapenta (small dry fish)
6 medium tomatoes
Olive oil
Salt
300g okra
206g kale green vegetable
¾ tsp sodium bicarbonate
6 tsp grounded peanut
400g super maize meal
(or roller maize meal)

1. Cut up cabbage and 1 onion
2. Add 4 tbsp. oil, ½ tsp salt
3. Mix and fry under medium heat until soft
4. Meanwhile put kapenta into a dry pot and brown for about 3 minutes
5. Soak with 500ml boiled water to remove the salt ~5 minutes [If kapenta is bought "salted", rinse with water at least 2x to remove the salt]
6. Repeat soak and wash thoroughly in the water rubbing in between the hands to remove debris
7. Put frying pan on fire, add 8 tbsp. oil until brown
8. Add 1 chopped onion and fry until onion pieces are brown
9. Add chopped tomatoes and fry until soft
10. Add kapenta into frying pan and leave on until water dries up
11. Wash kale, put in pot with 200ml water and bring to boil
12. Slice 1 onion into small pieces with 2 tomatoes and add to boiled kale
13. Add ½ tsp salt and mix thoroughly, cover and simmer for 5 minutes
14. Add ¼ tsp sodium bicarbonate, grounded peanut and 200ml water
15. Okra: Cut into a pot
16. Add 200ml water, ½ sodium bicarbonate, 2 chopped tomatoes, ½ tsp salt
17. Boil for ~10 minutes
18. At the same time put 1½L of water to boil in a pot
19. Mix maize meal with water in a bowl to a smooth paste and add to the boiling water
20. Leave to boil for at least 15 minutes
21. Add more maize [100g each time] while stirring and turning with a wooden spoon until desire texture is obtained
22. Leave for 15 minutes, mix thoroughly and divide into small portions to serve.

 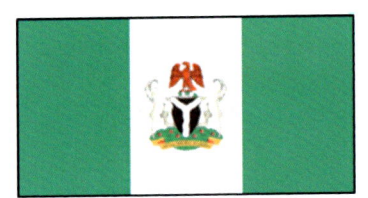 

MRS MARY BOLANLE ODOI

Yoruba Vegetable Soup

"Tete (Green-green) vegetable with fresh fish in spicy sauce"

This is one of the best Yoruba dishes. It is my favourite dish because my Grandmother loved it and she taught me how to prepare it when I was 10 years old. Before then I used to watch her and look at how she prepares the food. Between 10 – 11 years, I started little by little under her instructions, until I became perfect. It helped me when I got to Boarding house in Secondary School, as I was able to do some cooking by myself.

Grandma taught me to respect other people, not to tell lies and to face my studies. In addition, how a woman should look after herself and most importantly a woman should always be clean. Whenever I am giving advice to my children, I refer to Grandma's training. Anytime I think of this food, I think of Grandma with good fond memories.

INGREDIENTS
Serves 4-5

800g tete (can use shoko or gbure)
2 medium fresh mackerel (or salmon)
Fish seasoning
1 tsp salt, ½ chilli pepper
3 medium red bell peppers
2 small onions
800g tin plum peeled tomatoes
100ml palm oil
300ml sunflower oil
Smoked prawns (optional)
20g ground crayfish
50g Iru (locust beans) photo
3 Maggi cubes
Amala powder

1. Pluck the leaves one by one and rinse with water
2. Boil in 3.2L water for 10 minutes with salt
3. Meanwhile, clean out the fish
4. Cut into slices
5. Season with fish seasoning, put in container and cover
6. Wash the bell peppers, deseed, slice and put in blender
7. Slice both onions into the blender
8. Add tomatoes, chilli pepper and blend mixture
9. Put 3 tablespoon red oil into a cooking pan and heat up for about 3 minutes
10. When hot add blended mixture and sunflower oil
11. Add Maggi cubes, cover and simmer for 15 minutes
12. Stir and check occasionally until the water dries out and oil floats on top of the mixture
13. Taste that mixture no longer taste of raw tomatoes
14. Add the pieces of fish, stir, cover and simmer for another 10 minutes
15. Add crayfish and locust beans while stirring
16. Wash boiled leaves under running water
17. Squeeze out all the water, make into a round ball and chop into shreds
18. 10 minutes later, add chopped vegetable leaves
19. Cook for 5 minutes

Cooking time ~ 1 hour

Serve with Amala.

Amala

1. Pour 800ml boiled water into a pot and bring to the boil
2. Add 5 wooden spoonful of Amala powder and stir vigorously
3. Add 100ml water, cover and leave for 2 minutes
4. Stir, turn and serve

 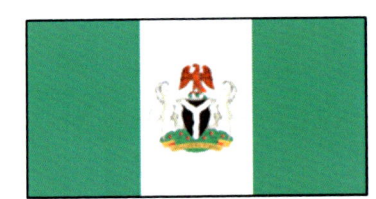 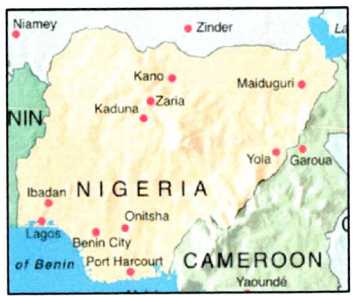

MRS ADESUWA OMOREGIE OGIE

Boiled Yam and Owoh Sauce

"A traditional soup from Edo State in Nigeria comprising of assorted meat in palm oil base sauce with potash"

I like this sauce because of the taste. It has a different and unique taste which is very pleasant on the taste buds My Mum taught me how to prepare this dish and she taught me many other dishes as well.

Whenever I cook it, it brings wonderful memories of her and back home. She always used to say, "pay attention because if you don't get it right, all will be wasted effort". I had to really concentrate on learning how to cook this dish.

Now I cook it when I am free and want to treat myself to something special.

INGREDIENTS
Serves 4
1 kg Assorted meat:
Liver, Tripe, Chicken wings
80g smoked dried giant Catfish fillet
2 x 400g tinned tomatoes
1 large onion
2 Knorr cubes
1 scotch bonnet pepper (optional)
3 tsp crayfish
1 tuber of yam 700kg
1 tsp salt
½ sugar
1 tbsp Groundnut oil
Palm oil
10mg Potash

1. Wash meat and put in a pot. Add water and boil for 40 minutes
2. Wash dry fish and add to the meat for the last 10 minutes
3. Blend:
4. 1 tin tomatoes, onion, Knorr cubes and pepper. 4 pulses and not too smooth
5. Add blended mixture to pot of meat
6. Rinse blender with 100ml water and add to pot of meat. Stir
7. Add crayfish. Stir
8. Leave pot open and cook for 10 minutes while the yam is being cooked
9. Peel the yam and cut into slices
10. Wash with water
11. Put into another pot and add 500ml water, salt, sugar and oil.
12. Cover and boil for 15 minutes
13. Coming back to the sauce
14. Crush potash on top of the sauce. This changes the taste of the sauce. Stir
15. Taste for saltiness
16. Leave for another 5 minutes
17. Turn OFF and allow to cool for 5 minutes BEFORE adding the Palm oil
18. Take out a portion of sauce
19. Add 1 tsp of Palm oil
20. 225ml palm oil was added to whole of pot

Cooking time ~ 1 hour

MRS OMOSEFE OHIREIN

Healthier Jollof Rice

"Healthy eating with brown rice and coconut oil"

This is one of my favourite dishes because it reminds me of special occasions during childhood, when my Mum would cook a pot of delicious Jollof rice. When leaving home to start my own family this became a dish I would cook to remind me of special times back home.

Being of the next generation, it was only right I took this recipe into the next generation, by using fab foods; brown rice and coconut oil. My family enjoy it and this will be my dish that I hope to pass on to my children.

p.s. Thank you mum

INGREDIENTS
Serves 4
420g (2 cups) Basmati brown rice (1 cup = 210g)
Water (4 cups - 2 cups of water per cup of rice)
300g chopped tomatoes
1 red bell pepper
1 yellow bell pepper
Medium sized scotch bonnet
1 large/2 medium sized red onions
1 tsp extra virgin Coconut oil
1 tsp Fish seasoning
1 Maggi cube

1. Place 2 cups of rice into a pot
2. Rinse rice in boiling water and drain
3. Add 4 cups of boiling water and place on hob to boil. Stir once
4. Reduce heat, cover and simmer for 15 minutes or until rice is partly cooked
5. While rice is cooking, finely chop 1 red onion, ½ red and yellow bell pepper and ½ half scotch bonnet pepper
6. Heat up coconut oil in a non-stick pot until fully melted
7. Add finely chopped ingredients
8. Add fish seasoning
9. While frying add remaining red and yellow bell pepper, scotch bonnet, 1 red onion and tomatoes, into a blender
10. Blend until the consistency is smooth
11. Pour this mixture into the hot pot of oil
12. Leave to fry for 10 minutes on high heat
13. Drain rice if necessary
14. Lower heat and pour in partly cooked brown rice
15. Add ½ cup of water. Stir with a fork
16. Add crushed Maggi cube
17. Leave to simmer for 10 minutes with lid ½ covered
18. Remove lid for last 15 minutes or leave on lowest heat until rice is cooked

Serve with your favourite meat, fish, plantain and vegetables or even enjoy it on its own

Cooking time – 45 minutes

MRS MARIE-ROSE OMOKHODION

Poisson Braisé

"Côte d'Ivoire's (Ivory Coast) famous grilled fish served with aromatic seasoning, tomato sauce and Attiéké"

This is an Ivorian favourite. Every young Ivorian girl knows how to cook it. My Mum taught me how to cook it and season it the right way.

The way it is cooked, the flavour, its international reputation, the freshness, the vinegar, the seasoning of the fish - to marinate it gives it the rich flavour. All of these make it an exquisite dish.

Just thinking about it brings me joy! It brings memory of home. Whenever I am home sick, through the cooking and eating of the dish – is like travelling home without buying a travel ticket……..

INGREDIENTS
Serves 6

3 x 610g Whole Tilapia
2 limes, juice of
4 medium fresh tomatoes
4 large red Bell pepper
12 tsp oil
2 limes, juice of
6 onions – diced
4 tsp chopped parsley
4 tsp diced spring onions
3 tsp crushed garlic
2 tsp chopped scotch bonnet pepper
6 Maggi cubes, crushed

2 tsp ground black pepper
12 tsp water
1 tsp ginger
1.2kg Attiéké
6 tbsp vinegar

1. Clean outside of fish by washing under running water. Take out everything inside
2. Slit the fish 3-4 times on each side
3. Cut lime into two. Drip the juice on top of fish and inside
4. Rinse with water and pat dry with paper kitchen towels
5. For seasoning: Mixture A
6. 6 tbsp onions, 3 tbsp parsley, 3 tbsp spring onion, 1 tbsp. garlic, 2 tbsp scotch bonnet pepper, 3 Maggi cubes, 1 tsp black pepper, 6 tbsp water, 3 tbsp oil and 1 tsp ginger. Blend until smooth in a blender
7. Using a brush, season the inside and outside of the fish
8. Put in oven at 200^0C for about 45 minutes. Turn half way in oven. Check to cook from cut on fish
9. Seasoning Mixture B
10. Same mixture as A plus 3 tomatoes, 3 red Bell peppers (seed included) and 100ml water. Blend to a smooth mixture
11. Put 6 tbsp oil in a pot. Make hot
12. Add tomato mixture. Cover
13. Increase to high heat until water dries up (about 25 minutes)
14. Taste for saltiness (Add ½ tsp salt if needed)
15. Add 3 tsp oil. Stir and cook for another 3-5 minutes
16. Take Attiéké out of freezer and defrost in microwave (1200W for 20 minutes)
17. Break into small pieces when cooked
18. Garnish:
19. 3 Maggi cubes, 6 tsp vinegar, Mix. Add 1 tsp black pepper, 3 tbsp diced onions (1 whole onion), 3 tbsp diced tomatoes (1 whole tomato), 1 tbsp fresh parsley, 1 tbsp spring onion (1 whole spring onion), 2 cloves of garlic, ½ red Bell pepper, optional ½ scotch bonnet pepper
20. Taste if palatable
21. Add 3 tbsp oil
22. When cooked, take fish out of oven and put on a flat plate
23. Pour garnish mixture over it

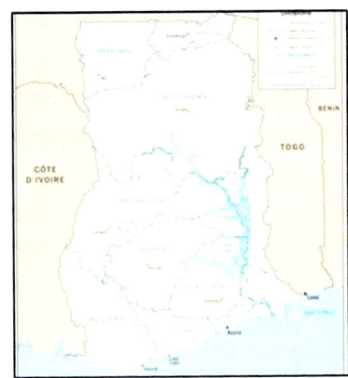

MR OPOKU OPARE

Palm Soup

"Assorted meat, crab and fish in a tomato based palm cream soup"

I like Palm soup because it reminds me of my childhood. I grew up in Accra, capital of Ghana by the sea. My grandmother's house was on the coast, which was beautiful. When we were naughty, we will be threatened by not going to grandmother's house. So when we get there, she says, "Today we're going to have 'League of Nations Palm soup'". She called it this because there is everything in the soup – assorted meat and fish except chicken.

I love cooking every day. I like fresh food. My two favourite things are cooking and ironing. By watching grandma, my mum and sisters, I learnt how to cook. My grandma taught me up to 6 ways to prepare okra stew/sauce. Because we lived on the coast, every Thursday we go to the beach James Town in Accra with Mum. We brought home different types of fish. While my sisters are cleaning the fish, my brothers would clean out the inside. It was fun time as the whole experience brought us close as a family.

INGREDIENTS
Serves 8

Assorted meat 2kg:	220g smoked mackerel
Tripe	Ginger/garlic paste
Cow's foot	Blackened Cajun
Lamb	2 medium onions
5 medium fresh tomatoes	1 Knorr beef cube
1 onion	450ml stock from meat
1 scotch bonnet pepper	Fufu
400g Palm cream	
300g crab	
Jumbo crayfish flavour	

1. Put the tomatoes, onion and pepper into a pot. Add 50ml boiling water. Cover
2. Bring back to the boil until the ingredients are soft ~ 10 minutes
3. Put ingredients into blender and blend but not too smooth
4. Add stock to pan
5. Add palm cream and start to boil
6. Add blended mixture and 250ml water to rinse out the blender. Stir and cover
7. Boil for 5 minutes
8. Add crab. Boil for 5 minutes
9. Add assorted meat
10. Boil for another 5 minutes with lid off. Stir
11. Cook at medium heat for another 5 minutes
12. Check for thickness. Add 1.5L water
13. Taste. Add ½ tbsp. crayfish seasoning
14. Cook at medium heat, ½ cover pot
15. The soup is cooked when all the froth disappears from the top of the soup. Stir from time to time
16. After about 25 minutes, split and remove bones from the fish. Add to pot
17. Lower heat from Gas mark 5 to 3
18. ½ cover pot for another 10 minutes
19. Once the oil is predominant on top of soup and no froth, then the soup is ready

Fufu (Serves 3)

1. Put 340g Fufu powder into a pot. Pour in 2 cups of hot boiled water
2. Stir to get a dowdy paste
3. Mash with wooden spoon for 2 minutes. Transfer to plastic container
4. Add ½ cup water on top of paste
5. Transfer to Microwave; 850W for 7 minutes
6. Transfer back to pot, stir and mash in pot
7. Knead the Fufu with your fingers and present the dish inside an "asanka" earthenware

Cooking time 1.5 hours

  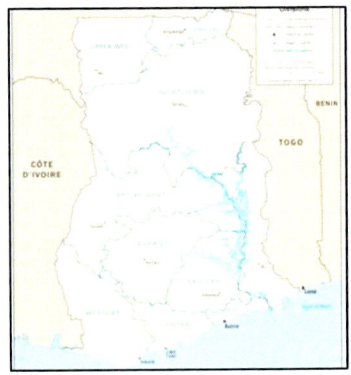

MR JOHN OQUAYE

Jollof Fried Rice

"A quick and healthy jollof fried rice with lots of vegetables and chicken"

I like Jollof fried rice because it is very easy to cook and make. Anyone can cook it. You do not need to be an expert. This is also a better alternative, an African inspired meal without the heavy oil based traditional way.

I am an African so in this fast-pace world we can find a way of treating our African based food in a quick to prepare way and to make it appeal to other nationalities. It has a Cosmopolitan feel.

I am a fussy eater and I have been cooking for myself since the age of 16. I like it my way, so I like preparing what I want to eat. I really do not mind cooking at home.

INGREDIENTS
Serves 6

4 cups Golden Basmati rice
1 cup water
1 tsp salt
10.9kg chicken pieces
1 Knorr vegetable cubes
1 Knorr chicken cube
5 tbsp olive oil
1 tsp garlic paste
1 tsp ginger paste
2 tbsp Pure creamed coconut
1 tsp Black pepper
140g Sun-dried tomatoes antipasto
400g Mediterranean veg mixture

180g Sundried tomato paste
1 tsp Hot pepper sauce
250g Pitted green olives
1 tsp chilli sauce
1 tsp Butter
116g Mix-vegetables
160g tomato puree
150g tomato passatta

1. 4 cups of rice , 1 cup water and 1 tsp salt in Tefal Rice Cooker for 30 minutes (Can use left over rice)
2. Wash chicken pieces and put in oven dish
3. Preheat oven for 10 minutes at 170^0C
4. In a cup: Mixture A
5. 5 tbsp olive oil, vegetable cube, garlic, ginger and creamed coconut
6. Microwave mixture for 1 minute - 900W
7. Stir and dissolve everything
8. Add 1 tbsp more olive oil and microwave for 30 seconds
9. Chicken pieces:
10. Sprinkle with black pepper, glaze with Mixture A
11. Put in oven for 45 minutes turning occasionally
12. Jollof:
13. Into non-stick pot add tomato puree, sun dried tomato
14. High heat for 2 minutes until its bubbling
15. Turn down to lowest heat
16. Add peppered sauce, 4 tsp of left over Mixture A
17. Add olives, chicken cube, sun-dried tomatoes cut into slices with a pair of scissors
18. Stir and take out any excess oil and add butter
19. Add rice into the tomato paste and stir
20. Add remaining olives and mix thoroughly
21. Increase heat and fry like stir-fry for 5 minutes
22. Can make it spicy by adding some pepper
23. Add mix-vegetable, cover and cook for 15 minutes under low heat
24. Taste for saltiness, add 1 tsp salt
25. Stir, cover for the last 5 minutes
26. Chicken pieces:
27. Half way, remove sauce, turn pieces over and baste with Mixture B
28. Chilli sauce, chicken cube and oil
29. Chicken pieces cooked after 45 minutes but can leave longer for crispy outer skin
30. Garnish chicken with Mediterranean vegetable mixture
31. Spread tomato passatta on top of the vegetables

Cooking time – 45 minutes

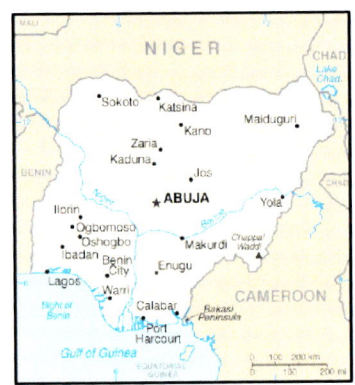

MRS LAUREL ORONSAYE

Coconut Rice

"A delicate preparation of rice in coconut and tomato based sauce with prawns and turkey meat"

This is my favourite dish because it is nourishing and delicious. I first ate it when I was a child when it was prepared by my mum. I learnt how to prepare it as a young girl back home in Nigeria.

Now when I prepare it here, it brings back memories of my childhood and ethnicity.

INGREDIENTS

Serves 10

162g Basmati Extra-long rice

400ml x2 Coconut milk

300g prawns

34g Smoked turkey meat

Vegetable/Rapeseed oil

Salt

1 tbsp thyme

3 pieces Bay leaf

2 Chicken Knorr cubes

400g chopped tomato can

2 onions

1 scotch bonnet pepper

1 red Bell pepper

2 cooking spoons sweet corn

2 cooking spoons peas

3 plantains

1. Slice one onion
2. Blend: chopped tomatoes, ½ onion and deseeded Bell pepper
3. Put 3 cooking spoonful of oil into a pot. Heat up for 1 minute
4. Fry remaining onion
5. Add 1 tbsp thyme, Knorr cubes, stir and lower the heat
6. Once the onions look softened , add blended tomatoes and cover
7. Increase heat to bring it to boil
8. When boiled, reduce heat from 6 to 3 (Electric cooker)
9. Add bay leaf
10. Add 8 cooking spoons of meat stock
11. Bring back to the boil
12. Once boiling, add prawns, sweet corn, and coconut milk. Stir
13. Bring to boil
14. Meanwhile wash rice with warm water 2/3 times until the water is clear
15. Drain properly after washing as the longer the rice is in water, the more likely for them to start breaking
16. Add the rice to the coconut stew in two halves stirring after each addition
17. Stir properly
18. Reduce heat. No more stirring after this stage.
19. Cover pot with foil paper to give an even cooling, Put the lid back on
20. Now, prepare some fried plantain as a side dish – to garnish the food
21. Turn over meat in oven
22. Add peas on top of the rice without stirring the whole pot – only try and get the peas into the sauce on top of the rice
23. Cover again with foil and cover of pot
24. Remove meat from the oven – after 45 minutes
25. Check rice – if not fully cooked transfer to an oven dish and into the oven maximum temperature for about 15 minutes
26. Preparation of fried plantains:
27. 3 plantains, peel off skin, dice into small pieces and fry in vegetable oil

Cooking time ~ 2 hours

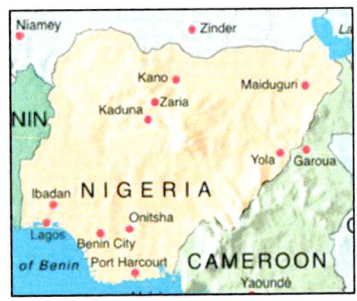

MR PHILIP ADE OTUBANJO (JP)

Ewedu Soup with Eba

"A soup that 'draws' with Ewedu leaves in palm oil with spicy fish"

I like the taste of Ewedu soup. We use to go from Lagos to Ijebu for holidays like Christmas in the 60s Great grandma used to prepare this as it was her favourite food. It had such a natural smell and everybody loved the taste.

I first ate it when I was about 8/9 years old in Nigeria when we went on holidays. I first prepared it here in the UK in 1985 but the problem then was buying the leaves and chopping them very finely – a time consuming process. Now, Ewedu leaves can be bought ready chopped. In addition, in the 80s, we had only semolina and ground rice, but now we have pounded yam, Fufu that go better with the soup.

Traditionally in the old days, they used Ewedu with very light ingredients – pepper and onions. Now it is just with garlic for health reasons. Ewedu is traditional for Yorubas and typical for Ijebu people.

INGREDIENTS
Serves 4
400g Ewedu leaves
100g smoked dried Tilapia fillet
1 tsp Cayenne chilli pepper
1 Maggi cube
1 glove garlic
3 tbsp Palm oil
2 tbsp Mixed crayfish and bongafish
1 tsp salt

1. Boil water. Ewedu 'draws' so be very careful not to add too much water
2. Pour 190ml into a cooking pot
3. Add cayenne pepper, palm oil, crayfish/bongafish mixture and garlic
4. Crumble one Maggi cube in a small amount of water to liquefy before adding to the cooking pot
5. Bring pot to the boil
6. Add ½ tsp salt. Stir
7. Meanwhile, soak Tilapia fillet in a bowl of boiled water. Add ½ tsp salt
8. Leave to soak for at least 5 minutes
9. Back to the cooking pot, add Ewedu leaves
10. Bring back to boil. Stir and cover pot
11. Check occasionally and stir so it doesn't stick to the bottom of the pot
12. After 5 minutes, rinse Tilapia fish and wash twice with water making sure there are no dirt inside the fish
13. Add fish to cooking pot. Stir
14. Reduce heat and simmer for about 10 minutes

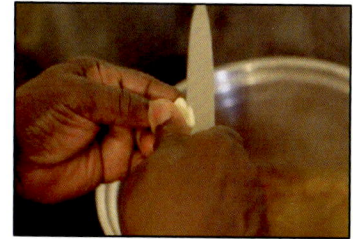

The water is the most important ingredient of the dish. Once it is watery – the soup is ruined.

Eat it with Eba or Pounded Yam

Cooking time – 30 minutes

  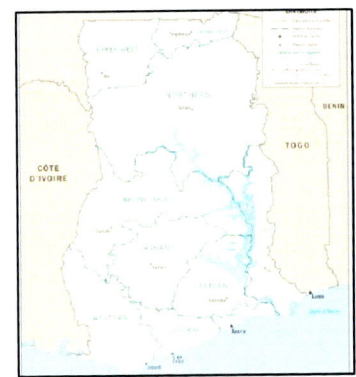

MRS BIBI OWUSU-SHADBOLT

ETO

"Mash plantain in palm oil with peanuts and boiled eggs"

This is our Royal food. It is food meant for a King or on a Special Birthday. It reminds me of my birthdays growing up in Ghana.

For birthday celebrations, the eggs on the dish represented the number of years of the celebrant before the advent of birthday cakes and candles.

INGREDIENTS
Serves 2
- 4/1kg plantains
- 4 medium size eggs
- 250g red onion
- 416g Avocado pear
- 1 Packet of peanuts – minimum 45g
- 1 tsp peanut butter
- 1 tsp salt
- Palm oil

1. Peel plantain and cut into pieces
2. Put into a pot containing 800ml of water
3. Add salt and boil for 30 minutes
4. Boil the eggs for about 15 minutes until hard and remove the water
5. Cut onion into 2 halves, slice one half into the wooden mortar
6. Add salt to make it easy to grind
7. Add handful (15g/0.5oz peanuts into the mortar)
8. GRIND
9. Add plantains – 2 lots each time and grind
10. Meanwhile put 25ml red palm oil into a frying pan
11. Slice the other half onion into the frying pan and fry the onions until brown
12. Use this oil to add to the mixture in the mortar 2 tablespoon each time
13. Add peanut butter to mortar and grind
14. Add palm oil
15. Add more boiled plantain
16. Continue until all plantain and oil have been added to the mortar to give a thoroughly mixed dish
17. Transfer onto a large plate
18. Cut avocado pear into oblong shapes and use to garnish the dish
19. Put one egg in the middle of dish and cut the others into nice shapes to garnish the dish
20. Sprinkle 2 handfuls of peanuts on the dish

Approximate cooking time: 45 minutes

  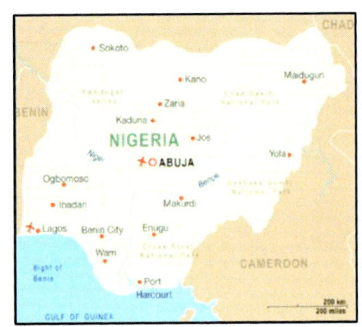

AROMA CUISINE (MRS ABIOLA REIS)

Aroma Mix

"Mixed vegetables in an aromatic stir-fry with yam and plantain"

This is a modern day quick and healthy meal for working parents with children. It is inexpensive to make and there is flexibility with the ingredients. For example, chicken can be used instead of prawns. Left over vegetables can be used which saves money and time. I have also included a healthier option.

I have used plantain and yam, which brings in the African cuisine. I love my African food and being able to mix it with ingredients that I can readily get in the shops here in the UK has turned out to be a satisfactory and good mixture for me and my children.

INGREDIENTS
Serves 6
10 large free range eggs
1 medium plantain 316g
1 yam 969g 10 slices
578g Mix vegetables
Sweet corn
132g sea sticks
142g prawns (optional)
1 medium Bell pepper – green/yellow/red
1 medium onion
Oil
2 tsp salt
1 medium size scotch bonnet pepper
2 Maggi cubes
1½ tsp All-purpose-seasoning

1. Peel and cut yam into 10 slices
2. Wash the slices and put into a pot. Add 800ml water
3. Peel plantain, wash and cut into 4 pieces. Add to yam in the same pot
4. Add 2 tsp salt. Cover and cook for about 40 minutes
5. While that is cooking
6. Into a bowl add mix vegetables, deseeded small size pieces of Bell peppers, small size pieces of scotch bonnet pepper, prawns, small size pieces of ½ onion and Maggi cubes sprinkled in
7. Add 200ml water. Mix thoroughly
8. Add 1 tsp salt. Mix thoroughly. Taste
9. Optional: Add 1½ All-purpose-seasoning
10. Mix thoroughly
11. Put in microwave, cover 5 minutes 900W [Don't overcook the vegetables]
12. Meanwhile, break eggs into a bowl. Beat
13. Add 1 tsp salt and ½ tsp All-purpose-seasoning
14. Beat and mix thoroughly
15. Frying Pan: Add 4 tbsp oil. Warm up oil
16. Add ¼ vegetable mix from microwave and sliced cut sea sticks
17. Fry for 3 minutes
18. Make sure vegetables are still crunchy – not soft
19. Transfer into a bowl and add ¼ egg mixture
20. Pour back into the frying pan
21. Turn over after 2 minutes to lightly fry the other side
22. Serve out on a plate and eat with bread

2nd Healthier Option
23. Use 1 tbsp oil
24. ¼ vegetable mixture, add diced sea sticks
25. Fry for 3 minutes
26. Add ¼ egg mixture on top. Mix until cooked – 3 minutes
27. This is better with yam and plantain as it has some liquid in it
28. After 40 minutes, drain away water from the pot of yam and plantain and serve with the fried mixture

Approximate cooking time: 40 minutes

Aroma Cuisine: +44 (0) 7801540833

MRS MODUPE OLANIBI ROBINSON

Ila-asepo

"Ogbono/okra soup with assorted meat from Ilesa, Osun State Nigeria"

This is my favourite food because the first time I tasted it was at my great-grandmother's house. I was 5 years old then. She came out of her hut to greet us, I was scared at first but immediately we went inside I could smell the aroma of the soup. The food was prepared in a clay pot. I cannot now remember the face of my great-grandmother but the taste and aroma of the soup, after 45 years still lingers on.

When I grew up, I asked my Mum to teach me how to prepare the soup. Now, I've also taught my children how to cook it.

INGREDIENTS
Serves 10-15
478g fish – mackerel
500g cow's leg
500g tripe
100g dry catfish
500g beef
526g okra
70g Ogbono
2 medium size onions
155g Kale vegetable
3 tbsp crayfish
2 cubes Jumbo seasoning/Maggi
13g Locust bean (Iru)
2 tbsp pepper
½ salt
7 tbsp palm oil

1. Put cow's foot, tripe and dry cat fish in a pot full of water and boil for 40 minutes
2. To 500ml water add the beef, jumbo cubes, salt,1 onion, boil for 30 minutes until soft
3. Add locust beans, pepper, 2 tbsp crayfish, 4 tbsp oil and boil for 30-40 minutes until soft
4. Taste for saltiness, add another cube of Maggi
5. Add fish (last to add in) and Ogbono
6. Leave to cook for 15 minutes with the pot open
7. Lower heat to low and simmer for 15 minutes
8. Meanwhile, add 3 tbsp oil into pot, heat for ~ 2 minutes
9. Add I chopped onion and fry for 5 minutes
10. Add okra, stir, add 1 tbsp crayfish and continue turning for another 5 minutes
11. Add to main pot of Ogbono mixture and stir
12. Wash vegetable and add to main pot

Serve with Pounded yam/Eba or Amala

Cooking time - 2 hours

Pounded Yam

1. 500ml cold water into pot and boil
2. Add 1 cup at a time of poundo iyan powder – 3 cups
3. Turn vigorously until smooth paste
4. Add 10ml hot water, cover and simmer for 5 minutes
5. Turn and stir for further 2 minutes
6. Ready to serve

This was how my great-grandmother served us 45 years ago!

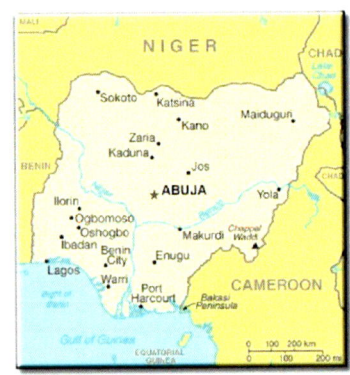

MRS YEMISI SIWOKU

Frejon and Akara – Yoruba style

"Coconut bean soup with fish stew and Nigerian bean cakes"

This is Lagos Isale Eko traditional dish for Easter. My aunty lived in Lagos while my grandmother lived in the village. On visits to Lagos, I stay with my aunty who taught me how to cook this dish.

The Lagosians that returned to Nigeria from Brazil at the abolition of the slave trade settled in an area now called "Brazilian Quarters" in Lagos Island. They brought this dish from Brazil. It brings back memories of a holiday adventure in my aunty's big house with cousins, a big family gathering on Good Friday, all in a big kitchen. It was like a treat to go to aunty's house! Now, my sons also like the dish and they will rather have it than beans on its own. So, they get the benefit of the protein of the beans.

As for Akara (bean cake) – My father has Akara every morning. We all had to learn from an early age how to prepare Akara for dad. It reminds me of days in the Boarding house when we use to buy them with freshly baked bread, over the fence from women sellers.

INGREDIENTS
Serves 2 - 3
335g brown bean
400ml tin coconut milk
2 tbsp. granulated sugar
½ tsp ginger
½ tsp garlic
1 Maggi cube
Salt to taste

For Fish Stew
1 small size onion
1 sliced onion
520g white fish fillet
20ml sunflower oil
1 medium red Bell pepper
1 scotch bonnet pepper
400g tomatoes
1 stick green onion
120g mixed pepper
½ black pepper
½ tsp thyme
½ tsp garlic
½ tsp ginger
2 Maggi cubes
Handful of Ijebu Garri

1. Soak beans overnight and rinse
2. Put in a pot, add 1760ml water, bring to boil on medium heat and cook for 2 hours until beans are very soft and mushy
3. Drain any water in pot and blend beans with 300ml coconut milk in a blender until smooth paste
4. Return to pot, add 100ml coconut milk, sugar, seasoning and simmer for 10 minutes while stirring to prevent sticking to bottom of pot
5. Fish stew: Pre-heat oven to 200^{0}C, put fish in oven dish and put in the oven. After 20 minutes, remove the water
6. Blend chopped tomatoes, red Bell pepper, onion, ½ scotch bonnet pepper with 50ml water
7. Add oil to frying pan, stir fry the sliced onions, spring onion, mixed pepper and ½ scotch bonnet pepper on low heat for 5 minutes
8. Add black pepper, thyme, garlic, ginger, Maggi cube and half of the blended tomatoes/pepper mixture (keep half in freezer for another day)
9. Cook for 15 minutes, add fish and cook for a further 5 minutes

Serve the Frejon with garri sprinkled over it with the fish stew
Cooking time ~ 45 minutes

Akara

1. Soak beans overnight in lots of water, drain and peel outside skin by rubbing in between your palms
2. Put peeled beans in blender; add ¾ onion, pepper and 150ml water. Blend and stop 3 times, until a smooth thick paste, feel and make sure it doesn't have bits
3. Transfer to bowl, mix thoroughly using a wooden spoon (this will make it to rise when fried), add salt and remaining diced onions
4. Put oil in frying pan, heat until hot ~3 minutes
5. Using a tablespoon, scoop blended beans and drop gently into the oil. Fry until golden brown on both sides, Press down with spoon to make sure its cooked inside
6. Remove to line paper towel to help absorb excess oil

INGREDIENTS
12 bean cakes
167g dried black-eye beans
1 medium onion
½ red scotch bonnet pepper
1 Maggi cube
1½ tsp salt
120ml sunflower oil

Serve with pap, custard, bread or eat as a snack

MRS VALERIE NKY TAIWO

Akara – Eastern Nigeria Style

"Fried Black-eyed beans paste fritters"

My favourite food is Akara – fried black-eyed beans fritters. However, I am going to prepare it as an accomplishment to healthy eating meal option with a twist of my Nigerian/African background to enhance flavour and provide added health benefits.

I grew up watching my mother who was a food contractor supply Akara for breakfast to a technical college in my hometown. I was the last child and I did not have any direct pressure to learn how to cook. However, I learnt in a most effective and loving way by simply being around my mum and watching her and sometimes participating in the stages of Akara preparation.

In addition, I went to market with her to buy ingredients as well as sell Akara. I watched her choose the right type of beans, peel the beans, slightly air dry it, grind the beans into paste, aerate the beans using a mortar, add seasoning and fry in the right oil and temperature. My mum's Akara was on high demand.

Akara is special…

Akara is one of the most versatile foods in Nigeria. It is eaten in all parts of Nigeria from the south to the north. It is called by names such as Kwoose, Akaraje etc. It is a great low cost business start up venture for most women. It is sold as a quick snack to travellers, as a street food for schoolchildren on their way to school and also on the table of the rich and famous as accomplishment to breakfast and lunch or dinner. It is also one of the foods eaten at naming ceremonies of most Yoruba people. It is usually accompanied with bread, cold water soaked garri, ogi – corn porridge.

Since living in the UK and becoming a qualified health minister, I have learnt to enhance Akara meals with raw vegetables salads and many other healthy options. This has given rise to a healthy inspired eating of my favourite food – Akara as my taste from Motherland for breakfast, lunch or dinner

Akara always remind me of my mum, who used her skills of making delicious Akara to make money, bought lands, built houses and helped so many people. So I jokingly tell myself to stay motivated in life because if mum used Akara to make riches, there is great hope for me.

INGREDIENTS
Serves 4
480g Black-eyed beans
2 medium size onions
¼ tsp cayenne pepper – optional
¼ medium scotch bonnet pepper deseeded
36g mixed coloured Bell pepper
Green/yellow/red
½ tsp Sea salt
500ml Rapeseed oil for deep-frying
Egg - optional

SERVE WITH

INGREDIENTS
Spicy Carrot Salad
6 medium carrots peeled, shredded or spiralled
1 lemon (juice)
3 tsp olive oil
1 tsb coarsely cracked chilli
Crushed Brazilian nuts or California currants
Parsley or chive for taste and garnish

INGREDIENTS
Confetti Root Vegetable Salad
1 small red onion
½ cup chopped red cabbage
½ cup chopped white cabbage
½ cup chopped cauliflower
½ cup chopped broccoli
½ cup chopped mixed coloured Bell pepper
green/yellow/red
½ cup diced celery
½ cup chopped parsnip
½ cup shredded kale
½ cup corn kernels
1 tbsp olive oil
1 medium size lemon (juice)
Pinch of salt
Cayenne pepper
Caraway seeds
Basil oil
1 cup = 125ml

1. Soak ready peeled beans in water (to slightly cover the beans) for 1 hour
2. Chop onions, pepper and place in bowls
3. Put beans, 42g onions, 20g red Bell pepper, scotch bonnet pepper into the blender.
4. Add 400ml water and blend until smooth (Water must be enough to just make a thick paste)
5. Pour beans paste into a bowl. Use whisk to whip the paste to aerate – 1 minute
6. Mix in cayenne pepper, sea salt to taste, 16g onions and 1 dessert spoon mixed peppers
7. Heat 500ml oil in a deep frying pan [Test with a small portion. Should pop up if oil is hot enough]
8. Use a table spoon to scoop beans paste into the oil, 2 spoons per ball
9. Deep dry until golden brown under medium heat
10. Flip balls for even frying
11. Reduce to low heat towards the end
12. Remove from oil with a large sieve spoon onto a plate lined with kitchen towel to drain oil

Cooking time - 1.5 hours

Serve with Spicy Carrot Salad or Confetti Root Vegetable Salad

Spicy Carrot Salad: Place carrot in large bowl, add pepper, crushed Brazilian nuts, add olive oil and squeeze in the lemon juice. Mix and toss in all ingredients. Serve with Akara and wholemeal bread.

Confetti Root Vegetable Salad: Place the ingredients into a large bowl and mix. Serve with Akara, wholemeal bread or baked sweet potato (wrapped in foil, baked at 200^0C for 1 hour).

Akara with fruits and vegetable – ½ coconut slices, mango cubes, grapes and cucumber slices.

Extract from "Let's eat the Healthy way – Step by Step Guide to maximising African recipes for health and taste!" By Valerie Taiwo. To be published soon.

MS FAY TAYLOR

Saturday Soup

"A sumptuous mixture of meat, herbs and assorted vegetables in a rich broth"

When I was young back home in Barbados, every Saturday we had soup. 'Saturday Soup Day'. My Mum always made it and it became one of my favourite dishes because it is wholesome due to the vegetables. I like vegetables.

I watched my Mum cooking it. When Mum moved back home and I fancied soup, I phoned her and got the recipe. I then added my own twist, I added corn-on-the cob because Mum did not put corn in hers. All family come together to have the soup

INGREDIENTS
Serves 2-4

460g Lamb neck
4 tbsp Vegetable broth mix
1 red scotch bonnet pepper
1 medium size onion
224g potato
50g cock flavour soup mix
50g pumpkin soup mix
2 gloves garlic
1 slice ginger
263g red sweet potato
246g white flesh sweet potato
316g Butternut squash   72g okra
518g yam   2 chicken stock cubes
396g cho-cho   10 sticks Thyme
463g corn on the cob 4 pieces   2 Spring onions
1 medium carrot   1 medium size onion

1. Add water to Lamb pieces in a pot, water just covering meat pieces
2. Bring to boil and discard water
3. Add 1L water, vegetable broth mix, scotch bonnet pepper, ½ chopped onion, crushed garlic, ginger

4. Cover. Put on high heat to boil. Then reduce to medium heat to cook (until meat is soft)
5. 30 minutes later add 1L water. Stir occasionally
6. Meanwhile, Prepare BATCH 1
7. Peel both red and white sweet potatoes and dice them into small pieces

8. Peel Butternut squash and use half of it
9. Peel yam and cut into small pieces
10. Transfer all to a large bowl of water.
11. Wash with cold water and leave soaking in the bowl of water
12. BATCH 2
13. Peel the cho-cho and de-seed. Dice and transfer into bowl

14. Peel carrots, wash and cut into slices
15. Cut off top and bottom of okra and cut into ½ remaining onion
16. BATCH 3
17. Wash spring rolls and cut into thin slices
18. Add 10 sticks of thyme
19. Dumplings:
20. Add 138g plain flour to 45g self raising flour
21. Put mixture in a bowl
22. Add pinch of salt, 2 tbsp brown sugar, ½ tsp brown sugar, ½ tsp grated nutmeg, ½ tsp cinnamon

23. Mix in a bowl
24. Add 100ml water gradually and beat using a fork, knead the flour mixture. Add more water and mix until into a dough – 115ml total
25. 45 minutes later, add chicken stock cubes to the cooking pot
26. 1 hour later, add ½ pumpkin soup mix, ½ cock flavour soup mix. Stir
27. Add 1L water, corn
28. Add BATCH 1, ½ thyme (take off stem and add the leaves) and spring onion. Cover
29. Cook for 10 minutes
30. Add BATCH 2 and 1 tbsp butter
31. Make dough into small balls and put into pot
32. Cooked 25 minutes later

Cooking time – 1 hour 40 minutes

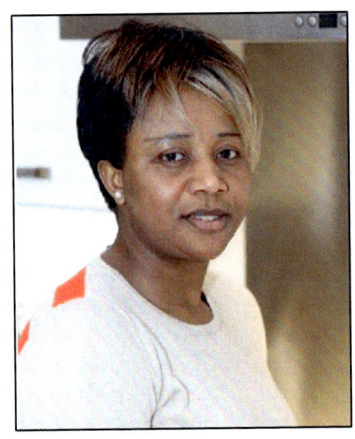

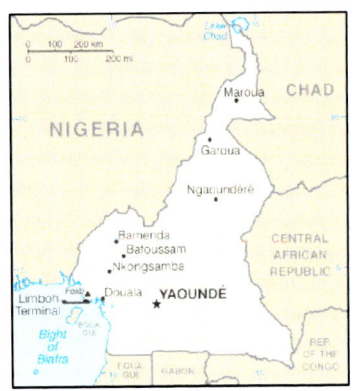

MRS REGINA TRIBUTH

Cameroon Pepper Soup

"Assorted seeds and nuts grounded to powder form and heated up with scotch bonnet pepper for a hot soup"

I like Pepper soup because it acts as an appetiser due to the spices. My grandmother taught me how to cook it. It is very useful to women who have just given birth as it helps to contract the uterus and clean out the womb.

I learnt how to cook it by watching my grandmother cooking while I was a child. Now, I cook it myself. This is my favourite dish and I like it because it gives me memories of the village back home. I like the taste and it stimulates my body especially during winter.

INGREDIENTS
Serves 2
250g beef meat
½ tsp salt
1 Maggi cube
Black pepper
26g Njasang (yellowish)
1 grain Bebe
1 medium size scotch bonnet pepper
½ tsp ground country onion

1. Wash pieces of meat and put in a pot
2. Add 1 cup 250ml water (enough to cover meat), salt and Maggi cube
3. Cook for 30 minutes
4. Add ground black pepper
5. Using the mortar: Put in Njasang and Bebe and blend together
6. Transfer blended mixture to cooking pot
7. Add scotch bonnet pepper that has been grounded in the mortar
8. Add country onion
9. Use more pepper to make it extra hot/spicy
10. Cooked in 25 minutes total time

MRS CATHRINE WARD nee Mahovo

Rice with Peanut Butter and Relish

"Basmati rice cooked in peanut butter sauce with chicken"

In Zimbabwe, we ate rice on special occasion and having peanut butter with the rice was like icing on the cake. I started eating it as soon as I could eat. It is a traditional dish because rice was not cheap then so it was a luxury eating it.

I learnt how to cook it when I was at Grade 5, aged 11 years. I was allowed to cook it using the traditional rice; which is different from the rice we have now.

This is my favourite food and when I eat it, it reminds me of Zimbabwe. It's nice, it's tasty and it makes me feel happy.

My Mum taught me how to cook, taught me about life, clean the house and to look after ones husband.

INGREDIENTS
Serves 4
1kg Boiler/Hard chicken
2 x 97g onions
477g (5) fresh tomatoes
2 tbsp oil
1 tsp paprika
1 tsp salt
4 cups Basmati rice
275g/1 handful Rapeseed leaves
4 tbsp smooth peanut butter

1. Cut chicken into small pieces and put into a large cooking pot. Fill pot with half full of water and cook for 1 hour on full heat
2. Cut onions into chunks
3. Remove all water from the boiled chicken pieces = 1.1L
4. Cut tomatoes into chunks with the skin on
5. Add oil to pot of chicken, add onion and paprika. Stir. Cook under high heat
6. Add tomatoes. Stir
7. Add some stock – 350ml
8. Taste for saltiness. Add 1 tsp salt (optional)
9. Cover – still under high heat
Rice:
10. Boil some water. Use cup = 150ml (1 cup of rice = 2 cups water)
11. 4 cups of rice plus 8 cups hot boiled water
12. Mix properly in the pot
13. Leave to boil and cook for about 12 minutes
14. Make sure the rice is cooked before adding peanut butter
15. Use a 'Magoti' an extra-long handle wooden spoon
16. For each cup of rice – use 1 tbsp peanut butter
17. Add peanut butter under medium heat stirring continuously for even distribution
18. Turn off soon after
Leaves:
19. Wash leaves and cut off the bottom stem
20. Cut into tiny, small pieces
21. Add 1 cup of water, cover and cook under low heat for 10 minutes
22. When cooked, make sure there's no water left in the pot. Add 2 tbsp peanut butter
23. To chicken pot, add 250ml stock
24. After 1 hour from beginning, check that the chicken is cooked by its softness

Cooking time – 1 hour 10 minutes

Glossary

The following are additional information about the ingredients and methods used in this cookbook.

AMALA
Amala powder is made by slicing yam, drying and grinding it into yam flour, which is then sieved and processed into Amala by mixing the powder into boiling water and stirring it to a desired texture. It is then served with a variety of soups. Popularly used among the Yorubas of Nigeria.

BEANS AND PEAS
This group includes black-eye beans, red kidney beans, black beans, pigeon peas and various coloured lentils. They are usually cooked together with rice or used in stews and soups.

BREADFRUIT
The name is derived from the texture of the moderately ripe fruit when cooked. Breadfruit is very rich in starch, which transforms to sugars when very ripe. Before it is eaten, the fruits are roasted, baked, fried or boiled. When cooked, the taste of moderately ripe breadfruit is described as potato-like, or similar to freshly baked bread.

CASSAVA
Cassava is a woody shrub native to South America but now found in most tropical and subtropical regions. The edible starchy tuberous root is long and tapered, with a firm homogeneous flesh encased in a detachable rind, about 1mm thick, rough and brown on the outside. The flesh can be chalk-white or yellowish. Cassava is classified as sweet or bitter depending on its level of toxic cyanogenic glucosides; improper preparation of bitter cassava causes a disease called konzo. Cassava is the third-largest source of carbohydrates for meals in the world. Nigeria is the world's largest producer of cassava.

COCONUT
Coconut is a large one-seeded nut of the coconut tree. When matured, it has a sweet tasting water middle, a hairy outside protecting a sweet thick white flesh from which coconut milk is extracted. It is chopped into small pieces and liquidised with little water and pressed through a sieve to extract the milk. Commercially made creamed coconut can be bought in 200g/7oz packets from supermarkets and grocery shops.

GARI
Gari or Garri is made from **CASSAVA** tubers. There are three types of gari: rough, medium and smooth. Each type is used for a particular meal. The rough gari is better used for soaking in cold water to drink usually with milk and sugar. The medium gari is cooked by adding boiling water and mixing vigorously to form a malleable soft paste called **EBA** in the Nigerian language. The smooth gari is usually mixed with pepper and other spicy ingredients with a small amount of warm water and palm oil in the hand. In West Africa, there are two varieties of gari: "white" and "yellow". The yellow being the gari fried with palm oil to give it an orange-like colour, while the white gari is fried without the oil.

OGBONO
Ogbono is the dried seed of the African mango tree and it is ground and used as a powerful thickener with an earthy flavour.
(Ref: Wikipedia)

Preparations: Eba (Page 15), Fufu (Page 57), Pounded Yam (Page 33), Maize meal (Page 47) and Amala (Page 49)